Campaign • 179

Sherman's March to the Sea 1864

Atlanta to Savannah

David Smith • Illustrated by Richard Hook

First published in Great Britain in 2007 by Osprey Publishing,
Midland House, West Way, Botley, Oxford OX2 0PH, UK
443 Park Avenue South, New York, NY 10016, USA
E-mail: info@ospreypublishing.com

A CIP catalog record for this book is available from the British Library

ISBN: 978 1 84603 035 2

Richard Hook has asserted his right under the Copyright, Designs and Patents
Act, 1988, to be identified as the Illustrator of this Work

Page layout by: The Black Spot
Index by Alan Thatcher
Typeset in Helvetica Neue and ITC New Baskerville
Maps by The Map Studio
3D bird's-eye views by The Black Spot
Originated by United Graphics, Singapore
Printed in China through Worldprint

07 08 09 10 11   10 9 8 7 6 5 4 3 2 1

For a catalog of all books published by Osprey please contact:

NORTH AMERICA
Osprey Direct, c/o Random House Distribution Center, 400 Hahn Road,
Westminster, MD 21157
E-mail: info@ospreydirect.com

ALL OTHER REGIONS
Osprey Direct UK, P.O. Box 140 Wellingborough, Northants, NN8 2FA, UK
E-mail: info@ospreydirect.co.uk

www.ospreypublishing.com

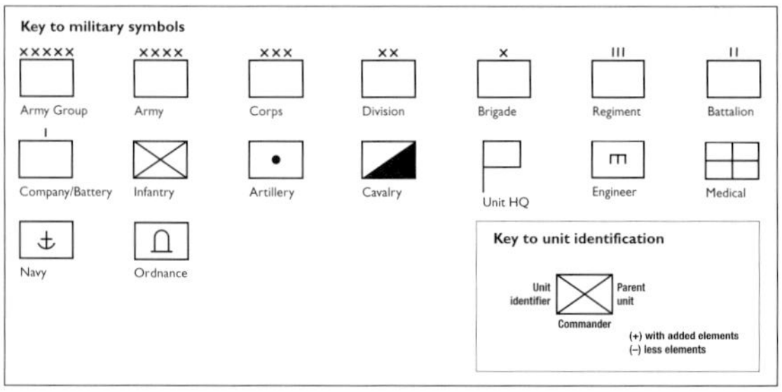

Dedication

This book is dedicated to my wife, Shirley, and our two
sons, Harry and Joshua.

Artist's note

Readers may care to note that the original paintings from
which the color plates in this book were prepared are
available for private sale. All reproduction copyright
whatsoever is retained by the Publishers. All inquiries
should be addressed to:

Scorpio Gallery
PO Box 475
Hailsham
East Sussex
BN27 2SL

The Publishers regret that they can enter into no
correspondence upon this matter.

Key to military symbols

XXXXX	XXXX	XXX	XX	X	III	II
Army Group	Army	Corps	Division	Brigade	Regiment	Battalion
I Company/Battery	Infantry	Artillery	Cavalry	Unit HQ	Engineer	Medical
Navy	Ordnance					

Key to unit identification

Unit identifier — Parent unit
Commander
(+) with added elements
(−) less elements

CONTENTS

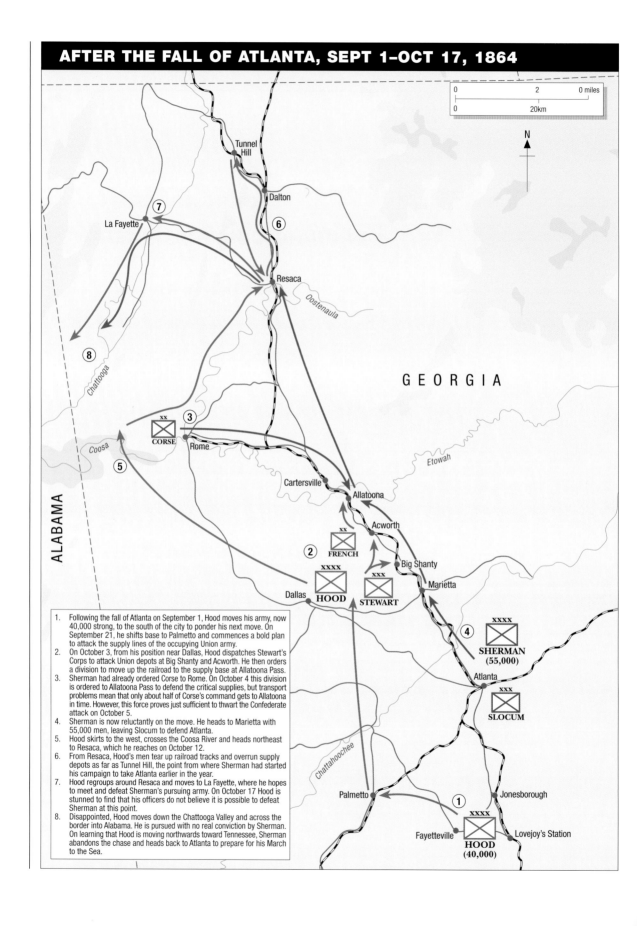

AFTER THE FALL OF ATLANTA, SEPT 1–OCT 17, 1864

0 — 2 — 0 miles
0 — 20km

N

Tunnel Hill

Dalton

⑦ La Fayette

⑥

Resaca

Oostenaula

⑧

Chattooga

GEORGIA

Coosa

xx
CORSE ③

Rome

⑤

Cartersville

Etowah

Allatoona

Acworth

xx
FRENCH ②

Big Shanty

xxxx
HOOD

xxx
STEWART

Marietta

④

xxxx
SHERMAN
(55,000)

Dallas

ALABAMA

Atlanta

xxx
SLOCUM

Chattahoochee

Palmetto

Jonesborough

①

Fayetteville

xxxx
HOOD
(40,000)

Lovejoy's Station

1. Following the fall of Atlanta on September 1, Hood moves his army, now 40,000 strong, to the south of the city to ponder his next move. On September 21, he shifts base to Palmetto and commences a bold plan to attack the supply lines of the occupying Union army.
2. On October 3, from his position near Dallas, Hood dispatches Stewart's Corps to attack Union depots at Big Shanty and Acworth. He then orders a division to move up the railroad to the supply base at Allatoona Pass.
3. Sherman had already ordered Corse to Rome. On October 4 this division is ordered to Allatoona Pass to defend the critical supplies, but transport problems mean that only about half of Corse's command gets to Allatoona in time. However, this force proves just sufficient to thwart the Confederate attack on October 5.
4. Sherman is now reluctantly on the move. He heads to Marietta with 55,000 men, leaving Slocum to defend Atlanta.
5. Hood skirts to the west, crosses the Coosa River and heads northeast to Resaca, which he reaches on October 12.
6. From Resaca, Hood's men tear up railroad tracks and overrun supply depots as far as Tunnel Hill, the point from where Sherman had started his campaign to take Atlanta earlier in the year.
7. Hood regroups around Resaca and moves to La Fayette, where he hopes to meet and defeat Sherman's pursuing army. On October 17 Hood is stunned to find that his officers do not believe it is possible to defeat Sherman at this point.
8. Disappointed, Hood moves down the Chattooga Valley and across the border into Alabama. He is pursued with no real conviction by Sherman. On learning that Hood is moving northwards toward Tennessee, Sherman abandons the chase and heads back to Atlanta to prepare for his March to the Sea.

ORIGINS OF THE CAMPAIGN

The year 1864 had once held great hope for the Confederacy. The chances of achieving a total military victory may have been slim, but there were other factors working in favor of the rebels. War-weariness in the North was increasing as casualties mounted and a presidential election was looming in November. There was a real chance that the Democrats might wrest power from Abraham Lincoln, and that in turn might mean a negotiated settlement to end the war.

One of Lincoln's former generals-in-chief, George Brinton McClellan, would run for the Democrats on a so-called "peace platform," while stories of savage fighting and terrible casualty lists made their way from the Wilderness, Spotsylvania, Cold Harbor, and the Siege of Petersburg to the pages of the Northern newspapers. Ulysses S. Grant, by now lieutenant general and general-in-chief, had hoped to win the war by the end of May, but as the eastern theater settled into a trench-bound stalemate, attention switched to William Tecumseh Sherman in the West.

Sherman's campaign against Joseph E. Johnston's rugged Army of Tennessee was a cat-and-mouse affair that saw clever maneuvering on the part of Sherman pitted against the careful defensive strategy of Johnston. Atlanta was Sherman's goal, and for a while it seemed Johnston would hold the Union forces at bay long enough to deny Sherman the sort of headlining victory that could reinvigorate the Northern war effort and save Lincoln. That all changed in July, when an exasperated Jefferson Davis, convinced that Johnston would eventually

Ever-growing casualty lists contributed to a mood of war-weariness in the North by the summer of 1864. A dead Union soldier at Petersburg, and a Confederate counterpart, bear silent testimony to the spiraling cost of the war – and with no end in sight, defeat for Lincoln in November's election was a real possibility. (LOC, LC-B811-3181)

give up Atlanta without a fight, replaced him with the impetuous corps commander John Bell Hood. Hood almost immediately attacked, but was beaten at Peach Tree Creek, Ezra Church, and Jonesborough. On September 1, Hood was forced to evacuate Atlanta. "Atlanta is ours," Sherman wired Lincoln, "and fairly won." Any talk of a negotiated peace was now unthinkable and Lincoln's re-election was a certainty.

Sherman was already making plans for his next move, and it was to be daring in the extreme. His anger at the South for starting the conflict revealed itself in a cold determination to make the people themselves experience war. He would force the civilian population to leave Atlanta, destroy everything of military value in the city, and then set out with his army on a march through Georgia, aiming for the coast, with the intention of destroying the state's war-making capability.

The plan was calculated and deliberate, but it was the end that interested Sherman, not the means. Removing Georgia from the rebellion might effectively be achieved by marching an army of 60,000 men right through it, but it might also be achieved by more subtle methods. Sherman made a bold offer to Governor Joseph Brown. If the governor withdrew Georgia from the rebellion, then Sherman's men would "spare the State, and in our passage across it confine the troops to the main roads, and would, moreover, pay for all the corn and food we needed." If not, he "would be compelled to go ahead, devastating the State in its whole length and breadth."

Sherman had not yet, however, received permission to embark on his bold march. There were many who considered a movement through hostile territory to be inviting disaster. Surely the Southern people would rise up and snipe at Sherman's isolated army at every opportunity, destroying foodstuffs, burning bridges, and whittling his men down until his army was entirely destroyed. Such apocalyptic visions were not uncommon, and even Lincoln and Grant were concerned. There was also the matter of Hood's army, situated around Lovejoy's Station and still a threat, especially given the unpredictable nature of the commanding

Confederate defenses around Atlanta may have proved difficult to crack, but Joseph E. Johnston's reluctance to attack the advancing Union armies under William Tecumseh Sherman would cost him his command. (LOC, LC-B811-2722)

With Atlanta safely in his grasp, Sherman turned his thoughts to the next stage of his campaign, but his plans to march his army through Georgia would not be well received by his superiors. (LOC, LC-B811-3626)

general. With 40,000 Confederates dogging Sherman's every step, the march might indeed become a nightmare for the Union general.

Events took an unexpected turn when, on September 21, Hood moved his army westward, to Palmetto, "thus," as Sherman saw it himself, "stepping aside and opening wide the door for us to enter Central Georgia." Sherman correctly assumed that Hood's intention was to attack the Union supply line – the railroad leading to Atlanta. It was an imaginative move from Hood, putting his army on the offensive after

THE BATTLE OF ALLATOONA PASS, OCTOBER 5, 1864
(Pages 10–11)

Allatoona Pass was a man-made railroad cut near the small town of Allatoona, which served as a major Union supply depot. With a garrison of around 900 men it was not a soft target, but nevertheless an attainable one for the Confederate division led by Samuel French. Overnight, John M. Corse hurried 1,054 Federal reinforcements to the scene, evening the numbers on both sides, and the situation was finely balanced on the morning of October 5. The main defenses were a pair of redoubts, including a star-shaped fort on the west side (1). French would concentrate his efforts here, and at 7.30am 11 guns under the command of Major John D. Myrick opened fire from the south side of the pass (2). Within an hour French had surrounded the Union garrison and issued an ultimatum – they were to surrender to avoid a "needless effusion of blood." Corse, living up to his cocky reputation, informed French that he was "prepared for the 'needless effusion of blood' whenever it is agreeable to you." A determined assault on the west side then saw the Union defenders driven from their rifle pits and into the fort, and Colonel William H. Clark of the 46th

Mississippi even reached the ditch in front of the fort, regimental flag in hand, before he was shot (3). Observing where the strength of the assault was falling, Corse called for reinforcements from the east side, where the action was less intense. Two regiments, the 12th and 50th Illinois, hurried down the hillside and crossed the railroad tracks to take up positions in the fort (4). Although the assault was becoming disorganized, it remained fierce. Corse was by now wounded after a bullet had grazed a cheek and ear, and ammunition was running dangerously low for the artillery in the beleaguered west-side fort. A volunteer scrambled across a wooden footbridge over the cut to gather as many canisters as he could carry, arriving back in time for his ammunition to blunt a further determined attack (5). French then received erroneous information that Union reinforcements were on the way and made the agonizing decision to break off the assault. He left more than 700 men behind. Sherman – in receipt of Corse's message that he was "short a cheekbone and an ear, but am able to whip all hell yet!" – would meet the victor a few days later and commented, on seeing the minor nature of Corse's injuries: "Corse, they came damned near missing you, didn't they?"

Alexander P. Stewart's Corps took the first action against General Sherman's line of communications, striking the railroad at Big Shanty and Acworth and forcing an exasperated Sherman to set off in pursuit. (LOC, LC-USZ62-12118)

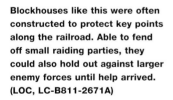

Blockhouses like this were often constructed to protect key points along the railroad. Able to fend off small raiding parties, they could also hold out against larger enemy forces until help arrived. (LOC, LC-B811-2671A)

months of retreat and defeat and taking the initiative from Sherman. With his own ideas not fully worked out and with no authorization from above, Sherman felt unable to ignore Hood's move. "If I felt sure that Savannah would soon be in our possession," he wrote to General Henry W. Halleck, Grant's chief of staff, "I should be tempted to march for Milledgeville and Augusta; but I must first secure what I have."

The first steps of Sherman's March to the Sea would have to wait. For now, he followed Hood, retracing the course he had followed so laboriously over the summer. Major General George H. Thomas was ordered to Nashville to organize that city's defenses, Sherman now believing that Tennessee was a possible destination for Hood. Then, leaving Major General Henry W. Slocum and XX Corps to garrison Atlanta, Sherman started north with 55,000 men. Hood got to work quickly. From his new base near Dallas, he dispatched an infantry corps under Lieutenant General Alexander P. Stewart, who quickly captured the Union garrisons at Big Shanty and Acworth and destroyed the railroad they were guarding. Stewart then sent a division under Major General Samuel G. French to take the major supply depot at Allatoona Pass. The transfer of ownership of a million rations was potentially a blow for Sherman, but he had made plans to resist Hood's movements. A division of XV Corps under Brigadier General John M. Corse had already been sent to Rome and he was now ordered to move his men quickly to Allatoona, 26 miles to the southeast, to reinforce the existing garrison of about 900 men under Lieutenant Colonel John E. Tourtellotte. Corse managed to deploy 1,054 men to Allatoona by dawn of October 5, but the remainder of his division was stranded at Rome following a train derailment. This left the two forces at Allatoona evenly matched, and the result was one of the most costly engagements of the entire war.

French's men forced the defending Union soldiers back into a star-shaped fort at the top of one side of the deep, man-made cut that dominated the railroad at Allatoona Pass. Determined attacks and even

Federal troops held the former Confederate defenses around Atlanta while Sherman's war of attrition against Grant was being waged. Having to give up Atlanta, the price for following Hood in Sherman's opinion, was too much for Grant to contemplate. (LOC, LC-B811-3637)

James H. Wilson would, in Grant's estimation, increase the effectiveness of Sherman's cavalry by 50 percent. The general-in-chief went so far as to suggest that Wilson could be turned loose in Georgia to accomplish Sherman's goal of destroying the war-making ability of the state, while Sherman's army tracked down Hood – a suggestion that did not find favor with Sherman. (LOC, LC-B813-2074)

more determined resistance resulted in losses of over 700 men on both sides – in proportion to the numbers involved the highest casualty rate of any battle in the entire war – before French called off the assault and withdrew. Corse, a flamboyant figure with an eye for the dramatic, suffered a minor wound when a bullet grazed his cheek and nicked his ear, but snapped off a defiant message to Sherman to announce his victory: "I am short a cheekbone and an ear," he wrote, "but am able to whip all hell yet!"

Hood had still greatly inconvenienced Sherman, and the extent of the damage wrought on the railroads is clear from Sherman's own assessment of what it would take to repair it: 6 miles of iron and 35,000 ties to replace the bent track and 10,000 men to do the work. Even so, in about a week the damage was repaired. "It was by such acts of extraordinary energy that we discouraged our adversaries," Sherman claimed, "for the rebel soldiers felt that it was a waste of labor for them to … burn a bridge and tear up a mile or so of track, when they knew we could lay it back so quickly."

Hood now crossed the Coosa River on October 10 and headed for Resaca, destroying more track as far north as Tunnel Hill, a psychological blow for the Union because this had been the point from which Sherman had begun his campaign to take Atlanta back in May. Hood would never be satisfied with attacking railroads, however. There must have been satisfaction in taking the offensive and enjoying considerable success at it, but he still believed he could beat Sherman. Moving his force to La Fayette, he awaited the approach of the Union army, intending to stand, fight, and defeat them.

Hood was not to get his battle, but not through any unwillingness on Sherman's part. Consultation with his corps commanders revealed to Hood that not one of them believed they could defeat Sherman. Realizing there was little point in forcing the issue, Hood moved down the Chattooga River Valley and crossed the border into Alabama. Sherman, disappointed that Hood had not offered battle, followed, but his efforts were now focused toward making his proposed march a possibility. On October 24 he sent Major General James H. Wilson, recently arrived from Virginia with Grant's personal recommendation, to Nashville with a large body of dismounted cavalry, keeping just a single division of cavalry with his own army. Sherman then ordered IV Corps to Chattanooga, where it would fall under the command of Thomas. On October 30 Sherman reconsidered and also sent XXIII Corps, under Major General John M. Schofield. With other troop concentrations nearby, and with two divisions of XVI Corps also on their way to Nashville, Thomas would have sufficient resources with which to take on Hood.

With Tennessee in good hands, the second stage of Sherman's plans was to convince Grant and Lincoln that the proposed march through Georgia was possible. Sherman was not finding this an easy task. "Do you not think it advisable," Grant wrote on November 1, "now that Hood has gone so far north, to entirely ruin him before starting on your proposed campaign?" This question might have given Sherman room to disagree, but Grant's message ended with a more direct order. "If you can see a chance of destroying Hood's army, attend to that first, and make your other move secondary."

Sherman was frustrated – he understood the futility of trying to catch Hood's army if Hood did not want to be caught. He was not shy about voicing his opinion, which he did most clearly in his reply to Grant on November 2. "No single army can catch Hood," he stated. "I regard the pursuit of Hood as useless. Still, if he attempts to invade Middle Tennessee, I will hold Decatur, and be prepared to move in that direction." Sherman then cleverly brought into the argument the consequences of such action: "but, unless I let go of Atlanta, my force will not be equal to his."

Sherman did not let Grant ponder this for long. On the same day he wired again: "If I turn back, the whole effect of my campaign will be lost," he pleaded. "I am clearly of opinion that the best results will follow my contemplated movement through Georgia."

This second telegram proved to be unnecessary. Grant replied to the first later that day. He had changed his mind. "With the force … that you have left with General Thomas, he must be able to take care of Hood and destroy him," Grant now believed. "I do not see that you can withdraw from where you are to follow Hood, without giving up all we have gained in territory. I say, then, go on as you propose."

Sherman had the permission he needed. He could now embark on his daring march.

General Grant's confidence in Sherman's ability was no doubt a powerful factor in his deliberations. Though he had doubts about leaving Hood to his own devices, and about Sherman's proposed march through Georgia, he eventually agreed to allow his trusted subordinate to put his plan into motion. (LOC, LC-B8172-6371 DLC)

CHRONOLOGY

1864

March 9	Grant becomes general-in-chief of US forces.
June 15–18	Grant's forces fail to take Petersburg and settle into a siege of the city.
June 27	Sherman is defeated at Kennesaw Mountain.
July 17	Hood is given command of the Army of Tennessee, replacing Johnston.
July 20	Hood takes the offensive against Sherman but is defeated at Peach Tree Creek.
September 1	Hood evacuates Atlanta.
September 21	Hood moves his army from Lovejoy's Station to Palmetto, setting out on his campaign to destroy Sherman's supply lines.
October 5	A Confederate division under French attacks the Union supply depot at Allatoona Pass.
October 17	Hood hopes to meet Sherman in battle at La Fayette, but his corps commanders are opposed to the idea and he heads towards the Alabama-Georgia border.
November 2	Sherman receives permission from Grant to embark on his March to the Sea.
November 8	Lincoln is re-elected as president.
November 15	XV and XVII Corps leave Atlanta and head towards Macon, screened by Kilpatrick's cavalry. XX Corps leaves Atlanta via Decatur, feinting on Augusta.
November 16	XIV Corps leaves Atlanta with Sherman in attendance, following the route of XX Corps.
November 21	Hood crosses the border from Alabama into Tennessee with 40,000 men and outflanks Schofield's 30,000-strong force at Pulaski.
November 22	The two wings of Sherman's army converge around Milledgeville. Walcutt's brigade (2nd Brigade, 1st Division, XV Corps) defeats a larger force of Confederate militia at Griswoldville.
November 28	Hood sends the bulk of his army to cross the Duck River, again outflanking Schofield, who just manages to get a division into Spring Hill to secure his line of retreat.
November 30	Hood attacks a strongly entrenched Schofield at Franklin, suffering losses of around 7,000 men. Despite the success of his defense, Schofield evacuates overnight.
December 1	Schofield reaches the sanctuary of fortifications around Nashville. Thomas now has a vastly superior force to Hood, but the Confederate commander nevertheless entrenches in the hills to the south of the city.
December 2	Sherman's forces reach Millen.
December 4	Kilpatrick, with the support of an infantry division, drives Wheeler from Waynesborough.
December 13	Hazen's 2nd Division, XV Corps, storms Fort McAllister.
December 15	After delays caused mainly by terrible weather, Thomas sweeps Hood's line aside on the first day of the Battle of Nashville, forcing the Confederates to retire and adopt a shorter defensive line.
December 16	The Army of Tennessee is routed on the second day of the Battle of Nashville and begins a long retreat, harried all the way by Thomas' victorious troops.
December 20	Confederate forces evacuate Savannah under cover of darkness.
December 21	Sherman's men enter Savannah, completing the March to the Sea.
December 26	Hood's exhausted men begin crossing the Tennessee River and the Union pursuit is called off three days later.

1865

January 13	Hood offers his resignation, which is accepted.
February 1	Sherman leaves Savannah and begins his march through the Carolinas.
February 17	Columbia, South Carolina, is burned by Sherman's troops.
March 19	Battle of Bentonville: Johnston fails to halt Sherman's advance.
April 2	Richmond falls.
April 9	Lee surrenders at Appomattox Court House.
April 26	Johnston surrenders in North Carolina.

OPPOSING COMMANDERS

UNION

Major General William Tecumseh Sherman (1820–91)

Sherman's character shines through clearly in photographs of this complicated, controversial figure. A somewhat disheveled, tense man who often exhausted companions by his mere presence, Sherman was restless and driven, seeking to end a war that he saw as illegal.

Born in Lancaster, Ohio, on February 8, 1820, and originally christened Tecumseh, he was adopted and rechristened by US Senator Thomas Ewing. He graduated from West Point in 1840 and married the senator's daughter ten years later. What Sherman termed a "vagabond life" saw him resign his military commission in 1853 and embark on a string of undistinguished business ventures. In 1859 he was installed as the superintendent of a military school in Baton Rouge, eventually to become Louisiana State University.

On the outbreak of war Sherman rejoined the US Army, suffering through accusations of insanity (the historian William S. McFeely claims that Sherman would today be termed a manic depressive), but crucially earning the respect and trust of Grant while leading XV Corps at Vicksburg and Chattanooga. Grant made Sherman his commander in the West when he assumed control of all Union forces. The campaign to take Atlanta was hailed by Grant as "the most gigantic undertaking given to any general in this war, and [had been accomplished] with a skill and ability that will be acknowledged in history as unsurpassed, if not unequalled."

Sherman's grasp of the nature of warfare did not sit well with many of his era and the distaste continues to this day. Variously hailed as a military genius or condemned as a war criminal, he nevertheless cut through the myths and romanticism of warfare to reach its core with one of his simplest but most resonant phrases: "War … is all hell."

Major General George H. Thomas (1816–70)

The "Rock of Chickamauga" played a crucial role in the March to the Sea, although he did not take a single step along the way with Sherman. Tasked with defending Tennessee, watching Hood's marauding army, and destroying it if possible, Thomas was the perfect choice to command the gathering Union forces at Nashville.

Born on July 31, 1816, in Southampton County, Virginia, he entered West Point in 1836, rooming with none other than William Tecumseh Sherman in his first year. After serving with distinction in the Seminole War and in Mexico, he returned to West Point in 1851 as Instructor in Cavalry and Artillery. He was to instruct, among others, a young Kentuckian named John Bell Hood. The Civil War forced Thomas into

William Tecumseh Sherman became defined by his March to the Sea. The North's avenging angel was the South's devil incarnate, his relish for the task revealed in a communication to Grant in which he insisted that he could "make the march, and make Georgia howl!" (LOC, LC-B813-6454A)

George H. Thomas' stolid nature comes across in this portrait. Famed for his stubborn defense at Chickamauga, he took his time to act at Nashville, but when he did he produced the only decisive victory of the Civil War. (LOC, LC-B813- 6480A)

John M. Schofield would do much to wreck the Army of Tennessee before it reached Nashville and might have completed the job himself at Franklin. He chose to withdraw, though he was quick to criticize Thomas' lack of action when he reached the safety of the lines around Nashville. (LOC, LC-B813- 1944)

an agonizing decision. He chose to remain with the US Army and was disowned by family and state.

Thomas would lay down critical groundwork for the Atlanta campaign at Chickamauga in 1863. His stubborn stand in command of the Union left, withstanding repeated assaults, saved the Army of the Cumberland from total collapse and earned him his nickname. It also enabled the US forces to keep their grip on Chattanooga, which was to be the launch pad for Sherman's campaign the following year, a campaign in which Thomas played a full part. Thomas was not without his critics, notably Grant and Sherman, who felt him more suited to defensive than offensive operations and doubted his ability to take the initiative against Hood in Tennessee. His decisive victory at Nashville was all the response he would ever need to such criticisms.

Major General John M. Schofield (1831–1906)

Born in Gerry, New York, on September 29, 1831, Schofield was already a famous soldier by the time he squared off against his old West Point classmate, John Bell Hood, in Tennessee. The recipient of the Medal of Honor for his part in the Battle of Wilson's Creek in 1861, Schofield had entered the volunteer service on the outbreak of the war, taking the post of Major of the 1st Missouri Volunteers in April 1861.

He advanced on Atlanta with Sherman and was sent north in command of XXIII and IV Corps to join forces with Thomas at Nashville when Hood embarked on his unorthodox campaign. His sparring with Hood was one of the most fascinating contests of the war, and Schofield emerged the clear winner, but he did not work well with Thomas when they finally combined forces, seeking to undermine his superior officer. After the war, Schofield served as Secretary of War from 1868 to 1869 and was promoted to lieutenant general in 1895. Perhaps his most notable postwar achievement was to propose that Pearl Harbor be adopted as a naval base.

Major General Henry W. Slocum (1827–94)

Born at Delphi, New York, on September 24, 1827, Slocum graduated from West Point in 1852, a commendable seventh in his class. A brief spell practicing law was ended by the outbreak of hostilities, when he became colonel of the 27th New York Infantry, fighting at First Manassas. A divisional commander at Second Manassas and Antietam, and a corps commander at Chancellorsville and Gettysburg, he was brought into Sherman's army to command XX Corps on the death of General James B. McPherson during the Atlanta campaign. On the March to the Sea he would have overall command of the left wing, the Army of Georgia, comprising XX and XIV Corps.

Slocum was respected enough as a corps commander, but he was not well liked as a person. There was a suspicion that commanding an army was a step too far for him, but a solid performance at Bentonville, during the march through South Carolina in 1865, redeemed him in the eyes of many.

Major General Oliver O. Howard (1830–1909)

Born in Leeds, Maine, on November 8, 1830, Howard graduated fourth in the West Point class of 1854. As a brigade commander he lost his right

arm during the Battle of Seven Pines, but he recovered and returned to service, earning command of XI Corps at Chancellorsville and Gettysburg. Poor performances in both battles put a question mark over his future, but he did well in the relief of Chattanooga and was given IV Corps for the Atlanta campaign.

McPherson's death made Howard the commander of the Army of the Tennessee – XV and XVII Corps, which he would lead on the March to the Sea as Sherman's right wing. A deeply religious man, he worked for the cause of African-Americans after the war and was a co-founder of Howard University in Washington, DC.

Brigadier General Hugh Judson Kilpatrick (1836–81)

One of the more flamboyant characters of the Civil War, Judson (as he preferred to be called) Kilpatrick was born in New Jersey on January 14, 1836. He graduated 17th in his class at West Point and was injured in his first action, at Big Bethel, on June 10, 1861. Joining the cavalry in December 1862 he earned a reputation for hard, sometimes reckless fighting and a fondness for the company of women.

An aggressive commander, whose penchant for driving both men and horses relentlessly earned him the dubious nickname of "Kilcavalry," he was famously described by Major James Connolly as looking "like a monkey" on horseback. He was nevertheless the sort of aggressive commander Sherman wanted leading his cavalry division on the March to the Sea.

CONFEDERATE

General John Bell Hood (1831–79)

Hood in some ways can be seen as representative of the entire Confederate war effort. A dashing, brave figure, he favored the offensive – at great cost. Seriously wounded at Gettysburg (where he lost the use of his left arm) and Chickamauga (where his right leg had to be amputated at mid thigh), his reputation is as an aggressive commander. This trait brought him his defining triumph, at the head of the Texas Brigade at Gaines' Mill, and also his defining failure, in Tennessee.

TOP, LEFT **The commander of Sherman's left wing on the March to the Sea, Henry W. Slocum, would enjoy his finest moment in the following campaign against rebel forces at Bentonville, South Carolina. (LOC, LC-B813-1876A)**

TOP, CENTER **Oliver O. Howard took control of Sherman's right wing. "Old Prayer Book" was not particularly popular with his men, but his personal courage was never in doubt – he had lost his right arm at Fair Oaks in 1862. Most of the fighting on the march would be done by Howard's men. (LOC, LC-B813-3719)**

TOP, RIGHT **A figure of fun for some, Hugh Judson Kilpatrick, known as "Little Kil," was nevertheless a bold and brave commander. "I know that Kilpatrick is a hell of a damned fool," Sherman commented, "but I want just that sort of a man to command my cavalry on this expedition." (LOC, LC-B815-340)**

19

TOP, LEFT **A haunted look in the eye of John Bell Hood bears testimony to the personal suffering he endured during the war. Losing a leg and the use of an arm, he remained an unpredictable, aggressive commander, whom Sherman was glad to see take command of the Army of Tennessee. (National Archives)**

TOP, RIGHT **Referred to as "that devil Forrest" by Sherman (something he no doubt took as a compliment), Nathan Bedford Forrest carved out an enviable reputation as a cavalry commander and is one of several Civil War generals credited with coining the phrase "I got there first, with the most men." (LOC, LC-USZ62-13705)**

Born in Kentucky on June 1, 1831, Hood was an undistinguished cadet at West Point, graduating 44th out of a class of 52. As a young officer in San Francisco he actually met Sherman, who was running a bank at the time, and was impressed by his "piercing eye and impulsive, nervous temperament."

When the war broke out his rise was meteoric – he became brigadier general on March 3, 1862, major general on October 10, 1862, and lieutenant general on February 1, 1864. Having persistently undermined his commanding officer, Joseph Johnston, during the defense of Atlanta, he was given command of the Army of Tennessee and the temporary rank of general on July 18, 1864. He was 33 years old. Hood's weakness was a failure to attend to the logistical details that came with running an army. His planning for the Tennessee campaign was sketchy at best, prompting alarm in his superior, Pierre Gustav Touton Beauregard, and he placed too much emphasis on the offensive, making his choice of title for his autobiography, *Advance and Retreat*, somewhat ironic.

Hood never led an army again after resigning command of the broken Army of Tennessee in January 1865, and he died, along with his wife and one of their children, during a yellow fever outbreak in New Orleans in August 1879.

Major General Nathan Bedford Forrest (1821–77)

Forrest was a brilliant cavalry commander, perhaps the finest ever produced by his country, and he earned a reputation as a military genius, although he had received no formal military training. A man of fiery temper, he was reputed to have personally killed 30 men, as well as having 29 horses shot from under him in battle.

A native of Tennessee, where he was born on July 13, 1821, he initially enlisted in the Confederate States Army as a private in 1861, but was soon a lieutenant colonel after paying for the formation of a mounted battalion. His first notable achievement was to escape from Fort Donelson with his battalion, the only men to escape from "Unconditional Surrender" Grant. By the middle of 1862 he was commanding a cavalry brigade in the Army of Tennessee and had risen to brigadier general by July of that year.

Though he lacked the dramatic flair of his adversary Kilpatrick, Joseph Wheeler nevertheless did all that could rightly have been expected with the small force at his disposal. His men earned a reputation for pillage that was second only to Sherman's bummers themselves, but they were formidable opponents in battle. (LOC, LC-B813-1974)

A falling out with his commanding officer, Braxton Bragg, led Forrest to request an independent command, which he received on December 4, 1863, along with the rank of major general. As a leader of cavalry raids he had no equal, and it is not surprising that efforts were made to pry him away from Hood in Tennessee in order that he might menace Sherman's advancing columns in Georgia. It is equally unsurprising that Hood declined such requests.

Major General Joseph Wheeler (1836–1900)

A Georgia native, Wheeler would lead the only serious opposition to Sherman's March to the Sea. Born in Augusta on September 10, 1836, he graduated from West Point in 1859 and, on the outbreak of war, entered the Confederate States Army as a first lieutenant in the artillery. He switched to the infantry with the 19th Alabama in 1861 and finally entered the cavalry's ranks in 1862. Rising quickly, he was a major general at the age of 26.

Wheeler was a small man, not much more than 120lb and much the same in stature as his Union counterpart in Georgia, Judson Kilpatrick, though far less flashy. A highly capable leader, he was, in the words of one of his officers, "as restless as a disembodied spirit and as active as a cat." He was wounded three times in action and legend has it he had 16 horses shot out from under him. Following the war he served as a Member of Congress and rejoined the army to command the cavalry in the Cuba campaign of 1898, at the age of 62.

OPPOSING ARMIES

UNION FORCES IN GEORGIA

Sherman wanted a lean, hard army for his march through Georgia. Consequently, an examination of each soldier was undertaken and any not coming up to scratch were sent to the rear, dispatched by railroad to Chattanooga. Sherman could not afford to be encumbered by sickly soldiers and his wagons were needed to carry food, forage, and ammunition. His army was therefore pared to, as one Union officer very aptly put it, "its fighting weight."

On November 10 all units taking part in the march were ordered to congregate on Atlanta. The army structure consisted of four corps which would be split into two "wings." The left wing, with Slocum in overall command, was made up of XIV and XX Corps, led by Major General Jefferson C. Davis and Brigadier General Alpheus S. Williams, respectively. The right wing, with Howard in overall command, was made up of XV and XVII Corps, with Major General Peter J. Osterhaus and Major General Frank P. Blair, respectively, commanding. The cavalry, led by Kilpatrick, would be under Sherman's control and would move from one wing to the other, depending on the actions of the Confederate cavalry under Wheeler.

The soldiers of Sherman's corps often made strange bedfellows. The Westerners of XIV Corps and the Eastern boys of XX Corps contrasted sharply. Having fought in a different theater to their Western compatriots, the men of XX Corps had different experiences to draw on and adhered to a stricter discipline than the often informal XIV Corps. The three divisions of XIV Corps added up to 12,953 officers and men, according to figures provided for November 10, with a further 399 artillerymen on hand. XX Corps, comprising three divisions, mustered 13,464 officers and men on November 10, with 632 artillerymen, giving the left wing a total strength of over 27,000.

XV Corps was the largest of Sherman's army, four divisions totaling 15,292 officers and men, with 387 artillerymen. Its partner in the right wing, XVII Corps, contained 11,087 officers and men and 271 artillerymen, split across three divisions, along with a small cavalry escort of 45 men. Total numbers for the right wing were therefore also over 27,000. Including Kilpatrick's 5,015-strong cavalry corps (a division in size), the aggregate strength of nearly 60,000 was ominous for the state of Georgia, with no large army on hand to resist.

Davis had led XIV Corps since he took over from Major General John M. Palmer during the Atlanta campaign. It had marched alongside IV Corps and XX Corps as part of the Army of the Cumberland, one of three armies under Sherman's overall command during that campaign. During the March to the Sea, XIV Corps and XX Corps became known as the Army of Georgia.

The commander of XX Corps, part of the left wing of Sherman's army, Alpheus S. Williams was a well-liked figure, popular with his men and fellow officers, though with a reputation as a hard drinker. Never a permanent corps commander, he nevertheless performed the task well when repeatedly called upon. (LOC, LC-B813-2179)

XX Corps had only been formed in 1864, fusing elements of XII Corps and two divisions of XI Corps with a new division, the corps being commanded by Major General Joseph Hooker. Most of the units in the new XX Corps had previously fought as part of the Army of the Potomac. Slocum was to take over after Hooker fell out with Sherman during the Atlanta campaign, and he in turn was replaced by Williams when Slocum assumed overall command of the Army of Georgia.

XV Corps was Sherman's old command, having been formed in 1862. In 1863, having lost its original 3rd Division, extra divisions from XVI and XVII Corps were added to bring the total to four. With Sherman's promotion, on October 27, 1863, to command of the Army of the Tennessee, Blair took over at the head of XV Corps. More reorganization came after the fall of Atlanta, with the 4th Division being split among the remaining three divisions and Corse's division of XVI Corps taking its place.

XV Corps, now under Osterhaus, was joined by XVII Corps (forming the Army of the Tennessee) for the March to the Sea and beyond. Two divisions of XVII Corps, the 3rd and 4th, had marched on Atlanta, being joined afterwards by Brigadier General John W. Fuller's division of XVI Corps (soon thereafter assigned to the command of Major General Joseph A. Mower) to bring its strength up to three divisions.

Morale among the Union troops was high following a long but successful campaign to take Atlanta. Faced with a march of indeterminate length to an unknown destination, the ranks were in something of a holiday mood at the outset of the March to the Sea. Sherman would later remember that "an unusual feeling of exhilaration seemed to pervade all minds – a feeling of something to come, vague and undefined, still full of venture and intense interest… There was a 'devil-may-care' feeling pervading officers and men…"

CONFEDERATE FORCES IN GEORGIA

The situation in Georgia as far as Confederate forces are concerned was fluid, making it difficult to make a definitive assessment of the units aligned against Sherman. The main opposition to the march would come from the cavalry under "Fighting Joe" Wheeler. Numbering around 3,500, the force was necessarily divided and Wheeler himself claimed never to have had more than 2,000 with him at any one time. Though of undoubted quality, these units could never hope to be more than an annoyance to an army of nearly 60,000 men.

Further units were often brought together to attempt a defense of a town or river crossing, only to be withdrawn and gathered at another position. A significant body of infantry from the Georgia State Militia (four brigades under Major General Gustavus W. Smith), together with two understrength regiments from the Georgia State Line, and a battery of the 14th Georgia Light Artillery, comprised a force of about 3,000 men that was stationed near Atlanta at the start of the march. They would offer resistance at Griswoldville and were finally part of the garrison of Savannah.

A total of about 10,000 men would be gathered under Lieutenant General William J. Hardee at Savannah, a conglomeration of units

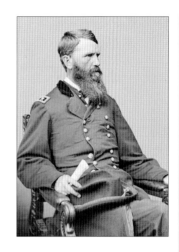

Despite being a "political general," Frank P. Blair, commander of XVII Corps in the right wing, had won the respect of his fellow officers. "There was no man braver than he," declared Grant, "nor was there any who obeyed all orders of his superior in rank with more unquestioning alacrity." Blair's corps was the first to enter Savannah at the end of the March to the Sea. (LOC, LC-B813-1704)

At the head of XV Corps was Peter Joseph Osterhaus. A German by birth, he had been trained in the notoriously draconian Prussian Army and arrived in the United States in 1848, eventually settling in St. Louis. He was promoted to major general during the Atlanta campaign. (LOC, LC-B813-1871A)

The epitome of the hard-drinking, hard-swearing, and hard-fighting soldier, Benjamin Franklin Cheatham was born in Nashville, which no doubt made Hood's campaign especially poignant for him. He took command of a corps in the Army of Tennessee when Hood replaced Johnston, but the persistent rumors of drink impairing his judgment on the battlefield would dog his career. (LOC, LC-B813-1975A)

Joseph Eggleston Johnston had led his army cautiously against Sherman in the Atlanta campaign, earning the devotion of his men. Hood, however, believed that the army had suffered from this careful husbandry and believed it had lost its fighting *élan*. (LOC, LC-B813-2109)

under the leadership of Smith, Major General Lafayette McLaws, and Major General Ambrose R. Wright. There were obviously huge problems attached to gathering forces together, and the nature of the units available, often inexperienced and in some cases mere cadets, lessened their effectiveness.

UNION FORCES IN TENNESSEE

Thomas was to assume overall command of the forces that faced Hood in Tennessee, but it took a while for the disparate Union elements to come together at Nashville. The major force, IV Corps and XXIII Corps under the command of Schofield, had been detached from Sherman following the fall of Atlanta and ordered northward when it became clear that Hood had designs on Tennessee. This army may have been small (numbering around 30,000 men), but it contained some of the most battle-hardened soldiers in the Union army.

Thomas also awaited the arrival of XVI Corps. Formed on December 18, 1862, this corps suffered more than any other from constant reorganization, breaking up, and consolidating. Two divisions were with Sherman during the Atlanta campaign, before being assigned to other corps following the capture of Atlanta. Under Major General Andrew J. Smith, the three divisions sent to Nashville numbered 10,280. The 1st and 3rd Divisions debarked from their transport vessels on November 30, with the 2nd Division joining them a day later.

A Provisional Detachment (District of the Etowah) under Major General James B. Steedman would bring 7,750 men within the Nashville lines. This detachment was made up of two Colored Brigades, along with a hodge-podge of units that had become detached from their regular divisions in the Atlanta campaign and had, for one reason or another, been unable to rejoin their official units.

The Post of Nashville added a further 2,027 men, and a sizeable cavalry corps, four divisions totaling 11,982 under the command of Wilson, brought the size of Thomas' command (present and equipped) to more than 56,000. The cavalry corps would be ineffective for some time, however, as the city was scoured for remounts, one of the major factors in delaying the assault on Hood.

CONFEDERATE FORCES IN TENNESSEE

Hood would cross the border into Tennessee with an army of around 40,000 men, including Forrest's cavalry. Organized into three corps (led by Lieutenant General Stephen D. Lee, Major General Benjamin F. Cheatham, and Lieutenant General Alexander P. Stewart), the Army of Tennessee was an experienced, disciplined fighting unit, having performed extremely well at Shiloh and Chickamauga, but one that was always in the shadow of the more successful and more famous Army of Northern Virginia.

The Army of Tennessee had numbered around 65,000 at the start of the Atlanta campaign earlier in the year. Under the careful command of Johnston, losses had been low as the army was pushed back by Sherman, but Hood lost 15,000 men in eight days upon taking over, highlighting the contrast between the two commanders. Confidence in Hood was therefore shaky at the start of the Tennessee campaign. There had been a spirit of sullen dejection among the men on Hood's appointment as general, but morale was restored by the advance against the Union supply lines and the return to Tennessee, home for many of the soldiers. That morale would be shaken again by events in Tennessee, but Hood's army would also display tremendous resilience in adversity.

Forrest's cavalry, numbering about 6,000, were among the best troops under Hood's command, but the Army of Tennessee would be without them at the crucial Battle of Nashville because of Hood's decision to send them to Murfreesborough. The smooth running of the Union assault of December 15 might have been disrupted had Forrest's troopers been present, and certainly the Union cavalry would not have had such freedom to operate.

The armament of the opposing armies was practically identical, although Union forces would enjoy the benefit of repeating rifles or carbines in two instances – in the second day of the Battle of Nashville and at the Battle of Griswoldville in Georgia. These were not decisive influences on events, however. In Tennessee the struggle would largely be like against like, with rifled muskets and artillery trading blows. The difference would come in the marshaling of forces. Hood's tactics would expose his men to withering defensive fire at Franklin, while Thomas concentrated his efforts (at least on the first day at Nashville) on out-flanking his enemy.

In contrast, the opposing forces in Georgia were so mismatched that the majority of Sherman's men had no need to call on their arms at all and, in a tragic parallel to events in Tennessee, it would be an ill-advised frontal assault against a prepared position that would bring the highest casualties of the campaign.

OPPOSING PLANS

UNION PLANS

The plans of the opposing armies were quite naturally shaped by the natures of the commanding generals involved. Sherman, who had a firmer grasp of the realities of modern warfare than any of his contemporaries, contrasted sharply with Hood, still fond of the frontal assault and searching for military glory. The result was plans that literally marched their respective armies in different directions.

Sherman believed that the population of the South must bear responsibility for starting the war. Only by experiencing the realities of warfare would they come to realize the full horror of what they had unleashed. He would march his army of 60,000 men through Georgia, aiming for Savannah but going wherever it pleased them, and nobody would be able to resist, let alone stop them. In modern military parlance, Sherman would identify more with the term "shock and awe" than with "hearts and minds."

The plan was simple, but that was its strength. Splitting the army into two wings, each of two corps, Sherman would be able to repeatedly threaten two targets at once. Confederate resistance, likely to be weak, would not be able to resist two movements at the same time and would

A park of about 200 wagons from the Eastern theater. Sherman's army would march with 2,500 wagons for supplies, and a further 600 as ambulances. The intention was to keep the wagons stocked with food and live off the land, destroying anything the army did not need. (LOC, LC-B817-7268)

have to choose where to defend. Sherman would then simply avoid the concentration of defensive strength and move on to threaten two more targets. The process would be repeated until he finally arrived at his destination, Savannah, where he would link up with US naval forces to resupply his army. The major military concern for Sherman was the cavalry force led by Wheeler, a highly capable commander. Sherman's own cavalry, flamboyantly commanded by Kilpatrick, was tasked with screening the advancing columns and keeping Wheeler at bay.

Equally important was the question of supplies. Sherman would take just 20 days' rations with him in long, snaking wagon trains. His intention was to "forage liberally on the country," with the dual aim of taking all his army needed and destroying all it did not. This destructive element of the march was at its very heart. Sherman had already admitted that he could keep his army under tight control and pay for whatever he needed, marching to the coast in an organized manner, but his offer to Governor Brown had been ignored. Now he would deliberately break the war-making ability of Georgia, and this included destroying buildings, livestock, and food supplies.

Each brigade on the march would provide organized foraging parties that would roam the flanks of the columns, meeting up again later in the day to unload their captured supplies. Inevitably, discipline could be lax in these parties and the "bummers" as they became known, would earn a reputation for vandalism and wanton destruction.

The possibility of the inhabitants of Georgia rising up against the invaders was a specter that haunted many in the North. It also had huge appeal for Southern leaders who had no other way of stopping the advance of Sherman's men. Jefferson Davis referred to a "retreat from Moscow" scenario, which would see the Union invaders enjoy the same fate that befell Napoleon, but in warm, abundant Georgia this was never likely.

CONFEDERATE PLANS

Sherman's plans would undoubtedly have been complicated greatly had there been an enemy force of 40,000 threatening to fall on his rearguard at any moment. Hood had removed this element from the equation, but Sherman was still very much on his mind as he prepared to launch his invasion of Tennessee. Hood believed that he could take on the scattered Union forces in Tennessee one by one, eliminating them, taking the city of Nashville, and forcing Sherman to reverse course and pursue him. It was not entirely fanciful, because Union strength was dissipated in the state. Much would depend on the speed with which Hood moved and how quickly he could dispose of each section of the congregating forces. If Thomas managed to bring all his forces into Nashville he would have overwhelming strength.

After taking Nashville, Hood also had dreams of crossing the Ohio, spreading panic in the North and eventually linking up with Robert E. Lee in the East, combining to smash Grant and win the war for the South. Few military historians have seen any basis of reality in this scenario.

THE MARCH TO THE SEA: PART 1

With Grant's approval for his march, Sherman immediately set about the detailed planning that would be necessary for such an undertaking. The four corps he would take with him needed to be concentrated at Atlanta. These corps had already been stripped of the ill and infirm, leaving only healthy, fit soldiers to march to the coast. Sherman was satisfied that the men Thomas had at Nashville, plus those on the way, were sufficient to deal with Hood and he was able to concentrate fully on his preparations.

There was the small matter of voting in the election, and state commissioners duly arrived to take the votes of the soldiers. At the same time, unwanted supplies were being transported away from Atlanta – Sherman's army would march light. Only one gun would be taken for each 1,000 men, with the artillery organized into batteries, usually of four guns each. Rations would be limited to a 20-day supply for the men and just five days' worth of forage for the wagon teams. Each man on the march would carry 40 rounds of ammunition, with 200 more per man in the wagons along with 200 rounds of ammunition for each gun.

The army may have been traveling light, but it still required 2,500 wagons, roughly 800 assigned to each corps, each with a team of six mules. There were a further 600 ambulances, each with a team of two horses, and yet more horses were required for hauling the guns. Sherman's wagon trains would wind along for 5 miles, enjoying the benefits of traveling by road while the infantry marched alongside. A large herd of cattle would supplement the men's diet, but would require more forage to maintain condition. It added up to a hungry army, one that would need to find additional food on its 285-mile journey to Savannah. In fertile Georgia, this was not expected to be a problem.

While Sherman's men were gathering at Atlanta, Colonel Orlando M. Poe of the Corps of Engineers was organizing the destruction of the city. This was carried out with such dedication that he was able to issue a succinct summation in his official report: "For military purposes the city of Atlanta has ceased to exist." The men of the Michigan and Missouri Engineers were instructed to destroy "all railroad and property belonging thereto; all storehouses, machine shops, mills, factories, &c., within the lines of the enemy's defenses at Atlanta. The work of destruction was thoroughly done... The designated buildings were first burned and the walls afterward razed to the ground."

The incoming troops were also laying waste as they marched to Atlanta, part of Sherman's deliberate campaign to "so damage the country as to make it untenable to the enemy." On November 12 Sherman received a message from Thomas, in which the usually restrained general showed an uncharacteristic flash of aggression, promising to "ruin" the Confederate army if they did not get out of his way. Sherman, eager to detach himself

Orlando M. Poe, tasked with destroying Atlanta prior to the March to the Sea, was the inventor of the "cant hook," a device used to twist rails after they had been heated over burning sleepers. Destruction was not his only talent, however. He also supervised pioneer battalions that achieved prodigious feats in bridge-building on this and subsequent marches. (LOC, LC-B813-1953A)

from the outside world, simply sent a brief acknowledgment and the telegraph line was cut. The moment was captured by Captain Charles W. Wills of the 103rd Illinois, who wrote that "The Rubicon is passed, the die is cast, and all that sort of thing. We to-day severed our own cracker line."

Sherman himself seems to have experienced an immense relief at being freed from the constraints of higher command, though he could not help but marvel at the "strange event" of "two hostile armies marching in opposite directions, each in the full belief that it was achieving a final and conclusive result in a great war."

By November 14 Sherman's army was in place. The two wings, XV and XVII Corps on the right and XIV and XX Corps on the left, had been issued their orders and knew that they had been organized "into an army for a special purpose… It is sufficient for you to know that it involves a departure from our present base, and a long and difficult march to a new one."

Sherman's Special Orders No. 120, issued on November 9, made it clear what was expected of the men. Each brigade was to organize a foraging party with the task of gathering supplies along the route of the march. The intention was to ensure that the wagon trains always had at least ten days' supply of rations for the men and three days' worth of forage for the animals. The foraging parties were forbidden from entering private property and only corps commanders were empowered to order the destruction of mills, houses, and cotton gins. This measure was to be reserved for areas where resistance was shown to the progress of the Union troops: "… should guerrillas or bushwhackers molest our march," Sherman instructed, "or should the inhabitants burn bridges, obstruct roads, or otherwise manifest local hostility, then army commanders should order and enforce a devastation more or less relentless, according

to the measure of such hostility." Foraging parties were instructed to always endeavor to leave families with enough food for their own needs.

The Federals would be marching through plantation country, and their actions would inevitably free large numbers of slaves. Sherman saw this as a potentially serious problem. He encouraged the taking on of able-bodied slaves to work in pioneer battalions, but otherwise freed negroes were to be discouraged from following the army.

On November 14, Poe was putting the finishing touches to his work in Atlanta when a serious fire broke out. A burning machine shop had been used as an arsenal by the Confederates and explosions appear to have started several fires, spreading quickly until large portions of the city were ablaze. In his report, Poe was at pains to insist that specific orders had been issued to his engineering parties that fires were not to be set until buildings had been demolished, "since it would endanger buildings which it is not intended to destroy." This contradicted his earlier report that buildings had first been burned and then razed. He claimed, however, that fires in the business district were caused by "lawless persons." This could just as easily have referred to Union soldiers acting on their own initiative, or to drunken mischief-makers, whether attached to the US Army or not.

Whatever the causes of the fire, it made an apocalyptic scene. Sherman himself did not leave the city until the morning of November 16, by which time three of his corps were already on the march. Atlanta was "smoldering and in ruins, the black smoke rising high in the air, and hanging like a pall over the ruined city." Sherman was a gifted writer,

TOP **A pall of smoke rises high in this artistic impression of the devastation of Atlanta. "Coming through Atlanta the smoke almost blinded us," wrote Captain Charles W. Wills of the 103rd Illinois, on November 13. "I believe everything of any importance there is on fire." (Harper's Weekly)**

BOTTOM **The March to the Sea commences. Atlanta still burns as Sherman's men set off for the coast. "We turned our horses' heads to the east," Sherman wrote in his memoirs, "Atlanta was soon lost behind the screen of trees, and became a thing of the past." (Harper's Weekly)**

and his description of the commencement of his march conveys the sense of expectation he and his men felt on cutting loose from all ties and striking off into the unknown:

> *Away in the distance, on the McDonough road, was the rear of Howard's column, the gun-barrels glistening in the sun, the white-topped wagons stretching away to the south; and right before us the Fourteenth Corps, marching steadily and rapidly, with a cheery look and a swinging pace, that made light of the thousand miles that lay between us and Richmond. Some band, by accident struck up the anthem of "John Brown's soul goes marching on;" the men caught up the strain, and never before or since have I heard the chorus of "Glory, glory, hallelujah!" done with more spirit, or in better harmony of time and place.*

THE MARCH TO THE SEA BEGINS

Sherman's men were on the move, in four great columns, with no serious opposition in the way. Wheeler's cavalry could harass, and would be a menace for isolated foraging parties, but Kilpatrick's Union horsemen would prevent them from doing any serious damage. The right wing, the first to move out on November 15, was moving towards Jonesborough, tearing up the railroad as it went. Kilpatrick was with them and saw action in the early going, Wills reporting that there was "quite lively skirmishing" over the first ten or so miles. Howard's wing was to head in the general direction of Macon, but its actual goal was to pass through the vicinity of the state capital of Milledgeville at the same time as the left wing, around November 22. The distance, 100 miles, and the time allotted to the march, seven days, would require a steady pace to be maintained.

On the left, XX Corps also departed Atlanta on November 15, Slocum leading his men to the east, through Decatur, towards Madison. By the time Sherman left Atlanta the following morning, with XIV Corps, the progress of the left wing was already threatening a move on Augusta, fulfilling Sherman's design of keeping the Confederates guessing as to their true objective. In fact, the Federal soldiers themselves had little idea of their destination, with the general consensus being that they were heading directly to Richmond to link up with Grant.

The progress of the left wing was unopposed. Sherman wrote of the night sky on his first evening out of Atlanta as lit by the bonfires of the crews destroying the railroads. The process was simple. A section of track would be pulled up, the sleepers arranged in a pile and the rails laid across the top. When the sleepers were set alight, the intense heat would soften the iron. The rails could be bent around the trunk of a nearby tree, or simply twisted – either method rendering the rail useless.

On November 17, XIV Corps arrived at Covington and marched through the town in some style, with bands playing and flags waving. The reception was cold from the white population, but ecstatic from the slaves. XX Corps was on its way to Madison when XIV Corps swung right the following day to head directly for Milledgeville.

Progress was equally rapid on the right wing, but here there was at least some resistance. Howard wrote of repeated skirmishes with rebel cavalry. At Lovejoy's Station, on November 16, Federal troopers drove off an enemy force, capturing 50 prisoners and two guns, while farther to the east the two infantry columns marched unimpeded to McDonough. Retreating Confederate cavalry could burn bridges, but the advancing Federals repaired them and continued their steady progress. Where necessary, pontoon bridges could be constructed in a matter of hours, each corps carrying a 900ft section.

The question of foraging was turning out to be a non-issue. If anything, there was simply too much for the army to cope with, and the wagon trains

River crossings were the main obstacles for the Union columns. Sometimes the pontoon trains were called up, but pioneer battalions would often construct new bridges out of local timber in double-quick time. In this artist's impression, XX Corps makes a crossing near Milledgeville. (*Harper's Weekly*)

of supplies were soon being viewed as an unnecessary hindrance by the men. "I wish Sherman would burn the commissary trains," wrote Wills on November 17, "we have no use for what they carry, and the train only bothers us… Our men are clear discouraged with foraging, they can't carry half the hogs and potatoes they find right along the road."

Spirits in the army were high, and the official foraging parties were enjoying such freedom that some disappeared for days on end, reveling in the absence of discipline while detached from the main army. Sherman was full of admiration for the work they carried out, although the Southern families whose land they crossed had different opinions. The foragers usually worked in groups of about 30 to 50 men, attended by one or two officers. They would leave camp before dawn and travel 5 or 6 miles, visiting each farm and plantation and taking whatever they could find, loading it onto requisitioned wagons and riding back to meet the marching columns on mules and horses. "Daily they returned mounted on all sorts of beasts," Sherman wrote with admiration, "which were at once taken from them and appropriated to the general use; but the next day they would start out again on foot, only to repeat the experience of the day before."

It was impossible to enforce discipline among the foraging parties, being detached from an army that was itself detached from the normal chain of command. Orders could be issued, but unless examples were made of those who crossed the line from foraging into wanton destruction, those orders would be ignored. Sherman had a chance to do just this early in the march, when a soldier not attached to an official foraging party passed close by him "with a ham on his musket, a jug of sorghum-molasses under his arm, and a big piece of honey in his hand, from which he was eating." The soldier, noticing Sherman, uttered to a friend, "forage liberally on the country," a remark which apparently earned laughter from some of the officers present. Sherman's response was merely to "reprove" the man, and remind him that foraging was to be undertaken only by the officially organized parties.

UNION FORAGING PARTY (Pages 34–35)

Sherman organized official foraging parties to scour the land on the route of the March to the Sea for supplies. As it turned out, there were more supplies than the foragers could cope with, or the 60,000 marching soldiers could consume. However, the parties were diligent in destroying whatever they could not carry, as their aim was also to destroy the war-making ability of the state of Georgia. The activities of the "bummers," as the foragers became known, would often cross the line into pure vandalism. This was exacerbated by the emergence of unregulated foragers, detached from any authority and sometimes even mixing with rogue elements of Confederate cavalry. Even with the "official" foragers, of course, it was impossible to maintain discipline as their regular units were so far away. Many houses were ransacked and personal belongings stolen, even though there were orders not to enter private dwellings (1). Although there was also an order to leave a family enough food for its own survival, this was often ignored, and many properties would be visited by several foraging parties over the course of one or two days. The fires set by the parties were mostly confined to storehouses and outbuildings rather than houses, but they made an ominous signal of the progress of Sherman's columns (2). The trail of destruction left in their wake instilled a hatred of the Union soldiers among the civilian population, but there was nothing they could do, although there are several reports of defiant Southern women berating the bummers (3). As well as its obvious sinister side, the foraging would often reach near-comical levels, as soldiers would dig excitedly at any area of freshly turned soil in the hope of finding valuables buried there by the family. The same patch would often be dug up repeatedly by subsequent parties, sometimes unearthing nothing more valuable than a dead dog (4). Vast amounts of livestock were taken, with foragers routinely leaving the Union lines on foot and returning at the end of the day mounted on mules or horses (5). The huge amounts of foodstuffs would be loaded onto waiting wagons in the Union columns and the process would be repeated the next day throughout the march to Savannah.

In fact, Sherman did not mind if his men crossed the line, within certain boundaries. Striking fear into the heart of the Confederacy was the intention of his march. "No doubt, many acts of pillage, robbery, and violence, were committed by these parties of foragers, usually called 'bummers,'" Sherman commented in his memoirs, "for I have since heard of jewelry taken from women, and the plunder of articles that never reached the commissary; but these acts were exceptional and incidental. I never heard of any cases of murder or rape."

This latter claim is ridiculous, of course. Sherman would later admit that he had been made aware of at least two rapes during the course of the march, and there were doubtless many more, as well as widespread theft, intimidation, physical violence, and petty vandalism. The foragers did not have everything their own way, however. By their nature they were isolated from the protection of the main army and thus vulnerable to bands of Confederate cavalrymen, who could be merciless. The bodies of 64 bummers would be found along the route to Savannah, enough to make them careful, but a mere pinprick to an army of 60,000. In fact, the Confederates were unable to offer anything more substantial. Wheeler's force was capable and well led, but numbering around 3,500 it was outnumbered by Kilpatrick's troopers, who also had the ability to call on infantry backup if pressed into a tight corner. Wheeler could do little more than hover around the flanks of the marching columns and try to pick off stragglers. The only other sizeable force between Sherman and Savannah was a collection of units, mostly Georgia militia brigades, under Major General Gustavus W. Smith. Numbering just 3,000, barely trained, and composed largely of those too young or old to have joined the regular army, they were no match for a comparable number of Sherman's veterans, let alone the vast force that marched through their state. Unable to do anything else, they fell back towards Macon.

THE CONFEDERATE RESPONSE

The reality of the march was perhaps a shock to some among the rebel ranks. Smith had seemed full of optimism on November 16 when he wrote to Wheeler, claiming that his militiamen had marched well, were in good condition, and would be "perfectly ready for anything that may turn up… If they [Sherman's soldiers] are not in largely superior force it is best for us to fight them here."

Just a day later Major General Howell Cobb, at Macon, was sensing the power of the oncoming columns: "Sherman's move upon this place is formidable, and the most dangerous of the war," he wrote to President Davis. "His policy is universal destruction."

The strategy for dealing with the invaders was built on vain hopes of some sort of popular uprising, and over-optimistic estimates of how Sherman's troops could be stopped in their tracks by greatly inferior numbers of defenders. Orders were issued to drive livestock away from the path of the advancing Federals, and to render mills useless. Hood, who had removed the only potentially effective obstacle to Sherman's advance, resisted calls to send reinforcements back to Georgia and implored Wheeler to "keep [your men] constantly harassing the enemy,

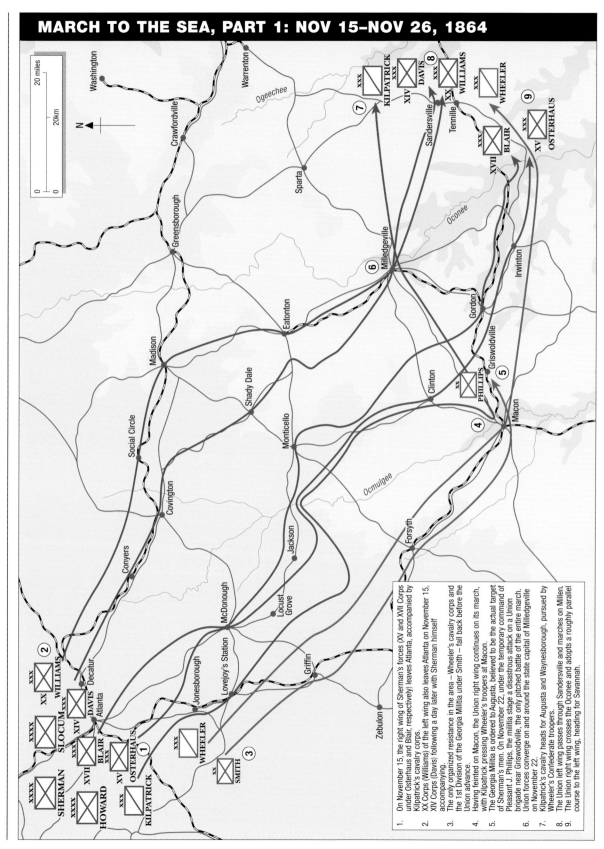

MARCH TO THE SEA, PART 1: NOV 15–NOV 26, 1864

1. On November 15, the right wing of Sherman's forces (XV and XVII Corps under Osterhaus and Blair, respectively) leaves Atlanta, accompanied by Kilpatrick's cavalry corps.

2. XX Corps (Williams) of the left wing also leaves Atlanta on November 15, XIV Corps (Davis) following a day later with Sherman himself accompanying.

3. The only organized resistance in the area – Wheeler's cavalry corps and the 1st Division of the Georgia Militia under Smith – fall back before the Union advance.

4. Having feinted on Macon, the Union right wing continues on its march, with Kilpatrick pressing Wheeler's troopers at Macon.

5. The Georgia Militia is ordered to Augusta, believed to be the actual target of Sherman's men. On November 22, under the temporary command of Pleasant J. Phillips, the militia stage a disastrous attack on a Union brigade near Griswoldville, the only pitched battle of the entire march.

6. Union forces converge on and around the state capital of Milledgeville on November 22.

7. Kilpatrick's cavalry heads for Augusta and Waynesborough, pursued by Wheeler's Confederate troopers.

8. The Union left wing passes through Sandersville and marches on Millen.

9. The Union right wing crosses the Oconee and adopts a roughly parallel course to the left wing, heading for Savannah.

destroying his trains, and cutting off his foraging parties." Beauregard, in turn, repeatedly asked Hood to send either men back to Georgia or assume the offensive in Tennessee immediately. Hood did neither.

Appeals to the populace took on an almost frantic tone. Beauregard, on November 18, wrote:

> *To the People of Georgia: Arise for the defense of your native soil! Rally round your patriotic Governor and gallant soldiers! Obstruct all roads in Sherman's front, flank, and rear, and his army will soon starve in your midst! Be confident and resolute! Trust in an overruling Providence, and success will crown your efforts. I hasten to join you in defense of your homes and firesides.*

The appeal to trust to an "overruling providence" was probably as practical as any of the other appeals in Beauregard's address. Confederate communications on the outset of the March to the Sea betray an impotence and rising alarm among the scattered and meager military forces: "Fourteenth Corps has reached Atlanta, giving Sherman four corps, fully 60,000 men"; "The enemy has burned Atlanta… He moved out of Atlanta with a very large force… We have no force to hinder him and must fall back"; "Enemy advanced with infantry, cavalry, and wagons early this morning. Have driven our cavalry back to this place"; "We are falling back rapidly… We are too weak to resist them unless re-enforced promptly"; "We are retreating as rapidly as possible"; "We have not sufficient force"; "Enemy pressing on rapidly."

A message from President Davis to Cobb revealed that this growing sense of desperation reached to the very top of the Confederacy. He asked that every able-bodied man be pressed into service, with slaves used to construct roadblocks. From Augusta, Brigadier General Gabriel J. Rains would be able to supply "shells prepared to explode by pressure" – landmines. "You have a difficult task," Davis admitted in a masterful display of understatement, "but will realize the necessity for the greatest exertion."

Meanwhile, the Union soldiers pressed on. It was, according to Captain Wills, marching with the right wing, "the most gigantic pleasure excursion ever planned." Under Howard the two corps progressed calmly towards

Pierre Gustav Touton Beauregard had once led the Army of Tennessee, before strangely leaving the Confederate States Army without informing anyone, citing ill health. On his return he distinguished himself in the defense of Petersburg, but he probably wished his old command was on hand in Georgia to resist the advance of Sherman's men. (From *Lee and his Generals*, by Augustus Tholey. LC-USZ62-135818)

Milledgeville, constantly screened by Kilpatrick's cavalry. The pontoon bridge was called for on November 18 when the wing reached the Ocmulgee River. Three hours after construction started, the men started to cross. A steep bank on the eastern side of the river made this a lengthy process and it was not until the morning of November 20 that the last elements of the wing's rearguard crossed. By then, rains were slowing the advance more effectively than enemy activity. The 4th Division, XV Corps, reported only minor corduroying of roads up to the Ocmulgee crossing – just 50 yards between McDonough and Jackson and 50 yards between Jackson and the Ocmulgee – but extensive corduroying afterwards as the rains turned the roads to mud. From the Ocmulgee to Monticello, 500 yards of corduroying; from Monticello to Hillsborough, 1,500 yards; from

ABOVE **President of the Confederate States of America, Jefferson Davis would be criticized for his decision to replace Johnston with Hood at the head of the Army of Tennessee, but he understood fully the importance of holding Atlanta and wanted a fighting general to defend the city. (LOC, LC-BH82-2417)**

ABOVE, RIGHT **Buildings in Madison burn as the Union left wing passes through. Widespread destruction would be limited to areas where resistance was shown by the population, but all buildings of potential military value were destroyed as a matter of course. (*Harper's Weekly*)**

Hillsborough to near Clinton, 1,200 yards; and from Clinton to Commissioner's Fork, 1,000 yards. The pontoon bridges were not always called for. At smaller crossings the pioneer battalions quickly constructed bridges from nearby trees, often completing the task before the pontoons were brought up. Between Monticello and Hillsborough one such crossing was improvised over the aptly named Big Muddy Creek.

These inconveniences barely held up the march, however. Macon still appeared to be the immediate objective of the right wing and to reinforce that impression Kilpatrick swung wide of the two infantry corps to threaten the town. Gustavus Smith's militia had retreated by rail to Macon as the Union troops had crossed the Ocmulgee, and they were entrenched about the town, but it was 2,000 of Wheeler's troopers who would first meet the Federals. Hardee, now in command of all Confederate forces in Georgia, had personally met Wheeler when the Confederate cavalry arrived at Macon on the night of November 19. The next morning, Wheeler received orders to advance from Macon to feel out the enemy's position. It was Osterhaus' XV Corps, moving through Clinton, that Wheeler first encountered, but it was Kilpatrick's men who pushed him back on Macon. A fortified line of dismounted Confederate cavalrymen was assaulted by Kilpatrick in his preferred style, the 10th Ohio Cavalry and 92nd Illinois Mounted Infantry leading the charge, but despite breaking through in some parts, the attack was not pressed. It was merely a feint, and there was no intention of seriously assaulting Macon.

Sherman's overall strategy had worked. The Confederates had concentrated what forces they had at Macon, believing it to be the first goal on the march. Now, as the Union columns moved on, there was confusion. The militia were ordered to head directly for Augusta, now believed to be the focus of the remorseless advance.

There had been much less activity on the left wing. The men of XX Corps had marched through Madison on November 19, to be greeted by ecstatic slaves who decorated the Union soldiers with roses as they marched by. Williams detached his 2nd Division, under Brigadier General John W. Geary, to destroy the railroad bridge over the Oconee River, while the rest of the corps swung southwards towards Eatonton and

Milledgeville, to be rejoined later by Geary's division. On the afternoon of November 21, Sherman found himself on a large plantation with XIV Corps. A box with the name "Howell Cobb" printed on the side revealed whose plantation it was and Sherman lost no time in acting:

> *I sent word back to General Davis [commanding XIV Corps] to explain whose plantation it was, and instructed him to spare nothing. That night huge bonfires consumed the fence-rails, kept our soldiers warm, and the teamsters and men, as well as the slaves, carried off an immense quantity of corn and provisions of all sorts.*

The wholesale destruction was in keeping with Sherman's philosophy that the rich landowners of the South were chiefly responsible for the war, and that the poor were generally neutral or actually pro-Union.

The following day, the left wing reached Milledgeville, and the first goal of the march had been attained. Confederate Brigadier General Henry C. "Harry" Wayne, with a force of just 650, wisely withdrew from the town. Various state officials and Governor Brown had already fled, and Sherman made his headquarters at the governor's mansion.

THE BATTLE OF GRISWOLDVILLE

While his plantation burned, Cobb was at Macon helping to organize the Confederate resistance. The militia had been ordered to Augusta and the 1st Brigade was already en route on the morning of November 22 when the 2nd, 3rd, and 4th Brigades, under the temporary command of Brigadier General (a Georgia militia rank) Pleasant J. Phillips, set off. With them were two understrength regiments from the Georgia State Line (around 400 men) and Anderson's Battery of four guns from the 14th Georgia Light Artillery. As the 3,000 or so men approached Griswoldville they caught up with another small body of Confederates, the 400 men of the Augusta and Athens battalions of the Confederate Reserve, under Major Ferdinand W. C. Cook. This rag-tag force was supposed to move directly for Augusta, but it stumbled upon a brigade of Union infantry – the 2nd Brigade, 1st Division, XV Corps.

Among the 1,500 Federals was Captain Wills and the 103rd Illinois. "We had a nice open field without even a fence on it, full 600 yards wide on our front," he would later write. Brigadier General Charles C. Walcutt, commander of 2nd Brigade, had ordered breastworks to be constructed, making the defensive position strong. Adding to their strength was the fact that many in the brigade were armed with Spencer repeating rifles. The atmosphere was relaxed and a meal was being prepared when the Confederates appeared. Inexplicably, Phillips lined his men up for an assault. He may have been emboldened by the realization that he outnumbered the Federals two to one, but his men were little more than raw recruits, while their opponents were seasoned campaigners.

The Union defenders fired the first shots of the day. A section of Battery B of the First Michigan Light Artillery, under Captain Albert F. R. Arndt, opened fire, but was soon under fire itself from the four enemy guns, a rebel shell immediately striking a caisson and forcing the Union battery to withdraw. Three lines of rebels were approaching, but

Jefferson Davis, commander of XIV Corps, was often greeted with frank astonishment when introduced, and sharing a name with the president of the enemy must have been a tiresome burden. He was rumored to be a "copperhead," a Southern sympathizer, but his sensitivity to an insult – he shot and killed his commanding officer during a quarrel in 1862 – probably kept any comments to a whisper. (LOC, LC-B813-2021A)

Charles C. Walcutt was in charge of the brigade that faced the Georgia Militia at Griswoldville in the only pitched battle of the campaign. A wound in the leg from artillery fire during the battle kept him out of service until March 1865, when he was able to rejoin his brigade. (LOC, LC-DIG-cwpb-07225)

Gustavus W. Smith was attending to administration when his command was led into a disastrous clash at Griswoldville. His official report stated: "notwithstanding my order to avoid an engagement at that time and place, a collision occurred, we being the attacking party, and though the officers and men behaved with great gallantry, they failed to carry the works of the enemy." (LOC, LC-USZ62-779)

the steadiness of the Union veterans told. Waiting until their enemy were within 250 yards, the defenders opened fire. "One after another their lines crumbled to pieces," Wills recounted. "It was awful the way we slaughtered those men." Bravely the rebels pressed on, but eventually they had to break, although they actually ran forwards to the protection of a ravine just 50 yards in front of the Union line. Walcutt was then struck by a cannon shot and Colonel Robert F. Catterson took command of the brigade. The Confederates were moving to the right, attempting to outflank the Union line. Catterson called for reinforcements, and there was also a real danger of running out of ammunition – the fast-firing Spencer rifles consumed huge quantities in blunting three determined Confederate charges and for a moment it looked as if the brigade would need to make use of its bayonets, because the inexperienced Confederates kept coming.

For three hours the small battle raged, until the rebels finally withdrew. The elation felt by the Union soldiers was tempered when they looked over the battlefield afterwards. "I was never so affected at the sight of wounded and dead before," Wills wrote. "Old gray-haired and weakly-looking men and little boys, not over 15 years old, lay dead or writhing in pain. I did pity those boys, they almost all who could talk, said the Rebel cavalry gathered them up and forced them in… I hope we will never have to shoot at such men again." Phillips' losses were estimated at between 1,500 and 2,000 by Union officers, a wildly inaccurate figure. Gustavus Smith, writing in detached terms of the disastrous encounter in his official report, mentioned a more likely figure of 600 killed, wounded, and missing. The 2nd Brigade suffered 14 fatalities and 79 wounded.

While this unnecessary and futile battle was being fought, XX Corps was destroying military supplies at Milledgeville. Williams reported 2,300 muskets and large quantities of small-arms ammunition, artillery shells, and gunpowder as being destroyed. For various reasons Milledgeville would become something of a watershed. From this point on the marching Union soldiers seemed to become more vindictive, the foraging more spiteful and destructive. Part of the reason may have been the discovery of Southern newspapers in the state capital, where exhortations to the public to rise up against the invaders could be read, though Sherman himself was not perturbed by the rhetoric: "Of course, we were rather amused than alarmed at these threats, and made light of the feeble opposition offered to our progress."

More rancor was created when, at a Thanksgiving meal, several emaciated Union soldiers appeared, having escaped from the notorious prison at Andersonville. Sherman's men knew well how much food there was in Georgia, and to see their fellow soldiers in such a condition angered them.

While the right wing continued on its way, the left remained at Milledgeville until November 24, destroying anything of potential military use, including "such public buildings as could be easily converted to hostile uses." The next aim for the left wing would be Millen, where it was hoped a large number of prisoners, most likely suffering like those at Andersonville, could be freed. Wheeler's Confederate cavalry had begun to move towards Augusta, so Kilpatrick's Union counterparts were called over to screen the left flank and keep Wheeler out of reach of the marching columns. On leaving Milledgeville, progress was steady to

The prison at Millen would be a target for Sherman's left wing in the second stage of the march. Though conditions in military prisons were generally appalling, it was usually more a matter of simple neglect than malicious mistreatment. (*Harper's Weekly*)

Confederate forces set fire to crops outside Sandersville, but were unable to hold their ground when both columns of the Union left wing arrived practically simultaneously. "A part of Wheeler's cavalry was hand-somely driven from the town by the advance skirmishers of the two corps," wrote Jeff Davis in his official report. (*Harper's Weekly*)

Sandersville, reached on November 26. Retreating rebel cavalry set fire to supplies before withdrawing, prompting Sherman to inform the towns-people of Sandersville that any further acts of defiance would be met with stern reprisals. The calls in the press for spirited resistance from the people of Georgia were therefore a wasted effort – resistance would only bring more misery and, with no substantial Confederate forces to defend them, their best option was to endure and wait for the Federal soldiers to pass by. This they did, at the rate of 12–15 miles per day.

The Oconee River was the next major obstacle for the right wing. Harry Wayne's small band, on its way to Savannah having evacuated Milledgeville, saw an opportunity to impede the progress of the long files of Union soldiers and mounted a resistance at a bridge over the Oconee. His force of about 650 (he estimated only 460 were actually fit for service) was composed of cadets, released prisoners, militia, and some cavalry and artillery. At the bridge he found 186 men, made up of a company of the 27th Georgia Reserves and a company of South Carolina cavalry, and two pieces of artillery. He was later joined by a detachment of the 4th Kentucky Mounted Infantry, sent by Wheeler. With this tiny, cobbled-together force he would oppose the advance of nearly 30,000 men.

Remarkably, Wayne's men held the bridge for nearly three days from November 23, when the first Union cavalry force appeared to attempt a crossing. "It is questioned if we get out of this pickle," he informed Major General Lafayette McLaws, part of the garrison at Savannah, at 1.00am on November 24. Later that day he requested more ammunition, reporting that his men were down to 25 rounds each. By November 25 he knew his position was hopeless, with the fear of being outflanked by the vastly superior force in front of him paramount, and in the early hours of November 26 he withdrew his small command. It had been an apt show of resistance, lacking nothing in bravery but everything in manpower, and it had accomplished little. Sherman was almost halfway to Savannah – and it had taken him just ten days.

HOOD'S TENNESSEE CAMPAIGN

While Sherman's troops were engaged on their march, Hood's Army of Tennessee was preparing to move on Nashville. Morale in the army was good – the advance through Georgia had gone some way to restoring the confidence of men who had been retreating for a long time, and now many of the soldiers were heading home.

Hood's plan has been dismissed by most as fanciful. It is true that success on the scale he imagined was unlikely, but there remained an element of sense in the scheme. Union forces in the area were scattered and if Hood's lean army could engage them before they converged at Nashville it might be possible to force Sherman to abandon his destructive march and chase Hood. The two corps Sherman had detached from his army were to be the first target. Under the overall command of Schofield, IV Corps and XXIII Corps, totaling around 30,000 men, were heading for Nashville to join up with Thomas. Hood's army would attempt to cut off the line of Schofield's march and destroy the two corps before they could reach their goal.

If the campaign was to be a race, Hood seemed unaware of the fact. He delayed starting his march for Nashville for three weeks, waiting for Forrest's 6,000-strong cavalry force to return from a raid on Johnsonville,

Nashville became a key supply hub for the Union by 1863. Five railroads carried goods into and out of the city, supplying Sherman's armies during the Atlanta campaign with, among other things, more than 40,000 horses, nearly 4,000 wagons and half a million pairs of shoes. It was a tempting target for Hood, but not a realistic one. (LOC, LC-B811-2651)

Tennessee. Having the cavalry was undoubtedly desirable, but moving should have taken precedence, as Beauregard repeatedly stressed in correspondence to Hood. On November 17 the assistant adjutant general, Colonel George W. Brent, informed Hood of Beauregard's concern, writing that "General Beauregard directs me to say he desires that you will take the offensive at the earliest practicable moment and deal the enemy rapid and vigorous blows, striking him while thus dispersed…"

The Army of Tennessee finally moved on November 21 with a strength of just over 40,000. Despite the delays, Schofield's force would soon be in grave danger. The Union troops had been stationed at Pulaski, from where it was believed a calm withdrawal to Nashville would be possible as the Confederates approached. Hood's army, however, moved swiftly and caught the Federals off their guard – Hood was on his way to Columbia to cut off the line of retreat before Schofield could get moving. In a desperate race, the 5,000 men of Brigadier General Jacob D. Cox's 3rd Division, XXIII Corps, reached Columbia first, securing the route for the remaining 11 Union divisions to follow.

During the night of November 27, Schofield crossed the Duck River and destroyed the bridges, entrenching his troops and awaiting Hood's next move. This was to take the form of an elegant flanking movement. On November 28, Hood would send a cavalry force to cross the Duck River upriver of Columbia, and follow this with the bulk of his infantry. Two divisions, as well as most of the Confederate artillery, would be left at Columbia under Lieutenant General Stephen D. Lee to bluff Schofield into thinking he was staying put.

The ruse almost worked. Schofield ignored repeated warnings on November 28 that Confederate forces were landing to the west, a heavy bombardment from the artillery at Columbia convincing him that Hood was intending to strike there. On November 29 Schofield again dismissed a warning from his cavalry that Hood's men had a pontoon bridge in place and were crossing the Duck in force. When Schofield finally acted it was half-heartedly. He dispatched Major General David S. Stanley with two divisions northwards – one division to be posted half way to Spring Hill and the other to proceed to secure the town – but he kept the remainder of his force rooted to the spot at Columbia, apparently transfixed by Lee's artillery bombardment.

Stanley proved to be the savior of Schofield's army. Hastening along the Columbia Turnpike on a parallel course to that of Hood's forces, but, critically, with the advantage of a macadamized road, he managed to move a brigade into Spring Hill (Colonel Emerson Opdycke's 1st Brigade, 2nd Division, IV Corps) just before Forrest's cavalry arrived. A brisk battle saw Forrest's surprised troopers fended off, giving time for the rest of the division to occupy the town. Fevered efforts were now made to make the position defensible.

Spring Hill was in Union hands, but the situation was still critical. Stanley, with one division of around 5,000 men, faced an entire infantry corps of double that number under Benjamin F. Cheatham. More Confederate soldiers were on the way, yet somehow events contrived to go wrong for Cheatham's men. An assault by Major General Patrick R. Cleburne's Division was ineffective, mainly because of confusion about the precise layout of the Union positions. Still, it seemed inevitable that, as more Confederates arrived, a second assault would break the thin

Stephen Dill Lee was a former artillery officer, having commanded the Confederate artillery at Vicksburg, so he was a good choice to oversee the diversionary bombardment at Columbia. The youngest lieutenant general in the Confederate States Army, he took over Hood's old corps when Hood replaced Johnston. (LOC, LC-USZ62-210890

David S. Stanley would lead the 2nd Division, IV Corps, on a desperate race to Spring Hill. "The Second Division was pushed on," he later wrote, and "drove off a force of the enemy's cavalry which … would very soon have occupied the town." His actions, so simply stated, very probably saved Schofield's army. (LOC, LC-B814-6473)

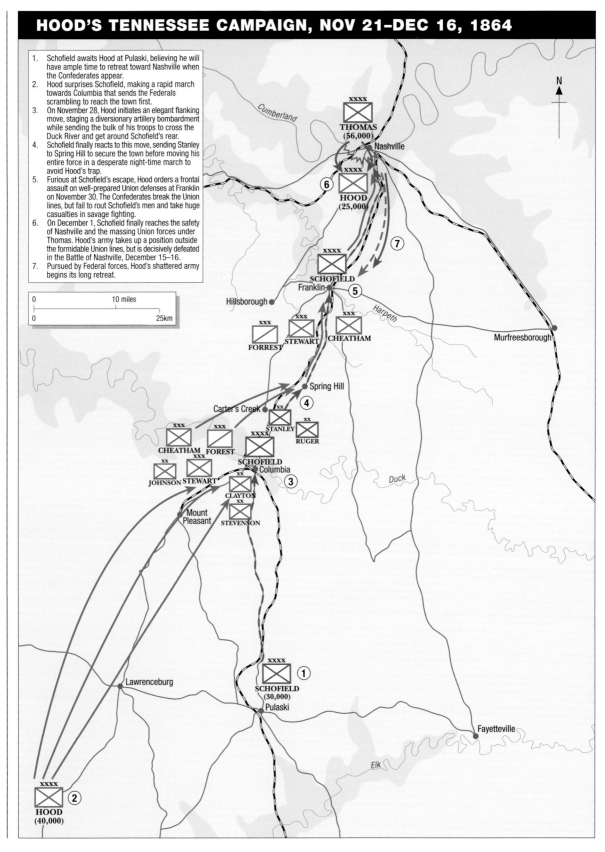

1. Schofield awaits Hood at Pulaski, believing he will have ample time to retreat toward Nashville when the Confederates appear.
2. Hood surprises Schofield, making a rapid march towards Columbia that sends the Federals scrambling to reach the town first.
3. On November 28, Hood initiates an elegant flanking move, staging a diversionary artillery bombardment while sending the bulk of his troops to cross the Duck River and get around Schofield's rear.
4. Schofield finally reacts to this move, sending Stanley to Spring Hill to secure the town before moving his entire force in a desperate night-time march to avoid Hood's trap.
5. Furious at Schofield's escape, Hood orders a frontal assault on well-prepared Union defenses at Franklin on November 30. The Confederates break the Union lines, but fail to rout Schofield's men and take huge casualties in savage fighting.
6. On December 1, Schofield finally reaches the safety of Nashville and the massing Union forces under Thomas. Hood's army takes up a position outside the formidable Union lines, but is decisively defeated in the Battle of Nashville, December 15–16.
7. Pursued by Federal forces, Hood's shattered army begins its long retreat.

N

0 ____ 10 miles
0 ____ 25km

Cumberland

XXXX
THOMAS
(56,000)

Nashville

XXXX
HOOD
(25,000)

⑥

⑦

XXXX
SCHOFIELD
Franklin

Hillsborough

⑤

Harpeth

XXX
FORREST

XXX
STEWART

XXX
CHEATHAM

Murfreesboro

Spring Hill

Carter's Creek

④

XX
STANLEY

XX
RUGER

XXX
CHEATHAM

XXX
FOREST

XXXX
SCHOFIELD
Columbia

XX
JOHNSON

XX
STEWART

Duck

③

XX
CLAYTON

XX
STEVENSON

Mount
Pleasant

Lawrenceburg

XXXX
SCHOFIELD
(30,000)
Pulaski

①

Fayetteville

Elk

XXXX
HOOD
(40,000)

②

This idealized painting of the Battle of Franklin, by the famous Civil War artists Kurz and Allison, nevertheless gives an impression of the close-quarter fighting that was to be such a feature of the desperate struggle. Hood's men would no doubt have looked longingly at the idealized depiction of their immaculate uniforms and boots as they attacked. (LOC, LC-USZC4-1732)

Union lines – but the second assault never came. In the gathering darkness Confederate soldiers stood and waited for the command to advance, but confusion and poor communications conspired and the attack never started.

Though bitterly disappointed that the town had not been taken, Hood knew he still had the advantage, having almost his entire force at Spring Hill while Schofield belatedly attempted to extricate his army from the trap. Now, however, it was Hood's turn to err. Confusion persists over the exact reasons why, but Hood failed to block the Columbia Turnpike into Spring Hill. While his men bivouacked within sight and earshot of the road, Union troops streamed past throughout the night.

Brigadier General Thomas J. Wood, then a division commander in IV Corps, noted how perilous the Union troops' position had been as they crept past Hood's entire army in the darkness: "The effect of a night attack on a column en route," he wrote, "would have been, beyond doubt, most disastrous."

Recriminations flew the next morning as the extent of the blunder became known. The best chance Hood could have hoped for had been wasted by a simple failure to attend to detail, and blame was freely offered in all directions. More ominous for his men was Hood's growing conviction that his army had gone soft. Suspicious of how the constant tactical withdrawals under Johnston had affected his men's fighting spirit, he saw Spring Hill as a confirmation that they were reluctant to attack a prepared defensive position. This was an injustice to his men, who were equally disgusted that they had not been sent against the Union positions. Brigadier General Daniel C. Govan later wrote that "a fatal paralysis seemed to have seized those in command."

Still fuming, Hood drove his disappointed and angry men after Schofield's withdrawing force, expecting them now to make straight for Nashville, but finding them at Franklin. This time, Hood would not allow the chance to engage Schofield's army to slip away. He would claim in his official report that: "The nature of the position was such as to render it inexpedient to attempt any further flank movement, and I therefore determined to attack him in front, and without delay." Almost as if he wished to punish his men for their failures, he resolved to mount a simple, head-on assault on the Union defenses.

Schofield's men had enjoyed a few hours' head start on Hood and had not let the time go to waste. Defensive works originally constructed in 1863 were repaired and strengthened and the position was enhanced by the ground to their front – it was almost totally unbroken for 2 miles. The Confederates would be marching across open ground, with almost no cover. Hood's subordinates feared for their men, but felt unable to mount any serious protest following the mistakes of the previous day. The assault would be led by Cheatham's Division and, having come in for especially bitter criticism from Hood after Spring Hill, he perhaps decided that strenuous opposition to the brutally simple plan would be unwise.

THE BATTLE OF FRANKLIN

Franklin nestled in a curve of the Harpeth River. The bulk of the Union forces were arranged in an arc around the outskirts of the town, with a division of IV Corps on high ground across the river in case the Confederates should make a crossing and once more try to cut off the line of retreat. To attack such a position was inviting huge losses, yet there was a weakness. The Franklin and Columbia Turnpike ran northward through the Union lines and presented a natural soft spot in the defenses. There was a gap in the breastworks, necessary for supply wagons to move through into the town, and although it was covered by artillery it was an obvious target.

Hood was so eager to attack that he was unwilling to wait for Lee's Corps, or the majority of his artillery, which were marching to join them from the diversionary action at Columbia. The decision threw away his numerical advantage, but delay would probably have enabled Schofield to withdraw his forces over the Harpeth under cover of darkness. As it was, Schofield fully expected to be able to do this. His engineers were repairing two bridges across the river and he did not expect Hood to attack, being far more concerned at the possibility of being outflanked if the rebels forded the Harpeth.

November 30 was unseasonably warm and calm, and Union soldiers prepared food while their officers chatted, flirted with local ladies, or simply dozed in the sun. Their reverie was broken by the appearance of 20,000 Confederate troops, aligned as if on the parade ground, with more than 100 regimental flags flying proudly. There was only an hour to go before sunset as the massive body of men took the first steps of the last great Confederate charge of the war. "It was worth a year of one's lifetime to witness the marshalling and advance of the Rebel line," was the opinion of a Union soldier who watched the Army of Tennessee march forwards.

There was little chance of success for the rebel soldiers, but Hood would once again be the beneficiary of a serious Union error. Brigadier General George D. Wagner's 2nd Division, IV Corps, had been left in an advanced position astride the Franklin and Columbia Turnpike, with orders to retire to the main lines when pressed by the enemy. What this advanced position could hope to achieve is uncertain, and confusion was so acute that one of Wagner's brigades, Opdycke's 1st, marched back into Franklin, apparently convinced that staying outside the lines could serve no useful purpose.

As the assault bore down on the Union lines, however, Wagner's men served a very useful purpose for the Confederates. Forced to stand by his orders (Wagner himself was within the main lines), they became fiercely engaged with the advancing soldiers of two Confederate divisions. Finally, about to be overwhelmed, the Union soldiers turned and ran back towards Franklin, half a mile distant, with rebel soldiers within 50ft of them. The panicked remnants of the two brigades acted as an escort as the Confederates approached the Union defenses, screening them until the awaiting defenders could wait no longer and a massive fire poured out against Confederate and Federal soldiers alike. It was too late to stop the momentum of the rebel charge and they kept moving. As the remnants of Wagner's command scrambled through the lines their officers called for them to rally in the rear. Some of the defending soldiers thought this was a general order and panic spread as the main line was largely abandoned. Opdycke, resting his men a few hundred yards in the rear, would write of a "most horrible stampede" of Union troops, a mixture of Wagner's shattered brigades and other defenders caught up in the confusion of battle.

From his vantage point across the river, Wood had no doubt that the battle was going disastrously wrong. "The enemy had come on with a terrific dash," he would write in his official report, "had entered our intrenchment, and victory seemed almost within his grasp." At the critical moment, however, further confusion saved the day for the Federals. Opdycke began to organize his men to meet the Confederate charge, but Major Thomas W. Motherspaw, of the 73rd Illinois, believed an order to counterattack had already been given. He led his men forward, apparently causing other regiments to spontaneously advance. Opdycke, unable to arrest the advance, instead uttered a simple instruction: "First Brigade, forward to the works!" Rallying other Union troops on the short march to the breach, Opdycke's men prepared to plug the gap, highlighting yet another mistake by Hood. His attack had been hastily put together and no reserve forces were available to exploit any successes. The Confederates who had stormed into the Union lines needed reinforcements to hold their position and solidify the advantage, but there were none. Opdycke's brigade was able to check the rebels and the initial crisis had passed.

The Battle of Franklin was not over, although any doubt about its outcome had been removed. Confederate forces would attack repeatedly, and Wood would write of "one of the finest, best contested, most vigorously sustained passages at arms which have occurred in this

The questionable positioning of George D. Wagner's (pictured) division at Franklin nearly had disastrous consequences for the Union forces. "The moment was critical beyond any I have known in any battle," commented his commanding officer, Stanley. (*Harper's Weekly*)

BATTLE OF FRANKLIN, NOV 30, 1864

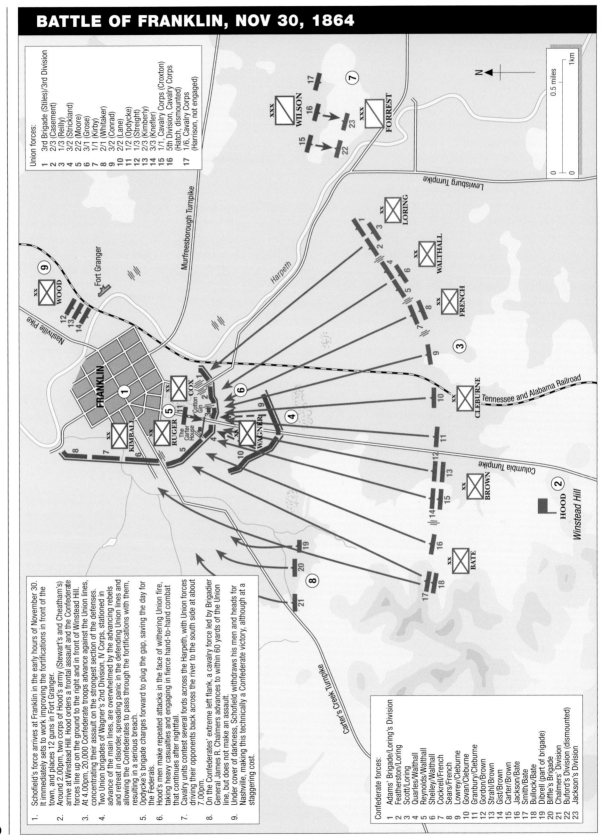

Union forces:

1. 3rd Brigade (Stiles)/3rd Division
2. 2/3 (Casement)
3. 1/3 (Reilly)
4. 3/2 (Strickland)
5. 2/2 (Moore)
6. 3/1 (Grose)
7. 1/1 (Kirby)
8. 2/1 (Whitaker)
9. 3/2 (Conrad)
10. 2/2 (Lane)
11. 1/2 (Opdycke)
12. 1/3 (Streight)
13. 2/3 (Kimberly)
14. 3/3 (Knefler)
15. 1/1, Cavalry Corps (Croxton)
16. 5th Division, Cavalry Corps (Hatch, dismounted)
17. 1/6, Cavalry Corps (Harrison, not engaged)

Confederate forces:

1. Adams' Brigade/Loring's Division
2. Featherston/Loring
3. Scott/Loring
4. Quarles/Walthall
5. Reynolds/Walthall
6. Shelley/Walthall
7. Cockrell/French
8. Sears/French
9. Lowrey/Cleburne
10. Govan/Cleburne
11. Granbury/Cleburne
12. Gordon/Brown
13. Strahl/Brown
14. Gist/Brown
15. Carter/Brown
16. Jackson/Bate
17. Smith/Bate
18. Bullock/Bate
19. Dibrell (part of brigade)
20. Biffle's Brigade
21. Jackson's Division
22. Chalmers' Division
23. Buford's Division (dismounted)
24. Jackson's Division

1. Schofield's force arrives at Franklin in the early hours of November 30. It immediately sets to work improving the fortifications in front of the town, and places 12 guns in Fort Granger.

2. Around 2.00pm, two corps of Hood's army (Stewart's and Cheatham's) arrive at Winstead Hill. Hood orders a frontal assault and the Confederate forces line up on the ground to the right and in front of Winstead Hill.

3. At 4.00pm, 20,000 Confederate troops advance against the Union lines, concentrating their assault on the strongest section of the defenses.

4. Two Union brigades of Wagner's 2nd Division, IV Corps, stationed in advance of the main lines, are overwhelmed by the advancing rebels and retreat in disorder, spreading panic in the defending Union lines and allowing the Confederates to pass through the fortifications with them, resulting in a serious breach.

5. Opdycke's brigade charges forward to plug the gap, saving the day for the Federals.

6. Hood's men make repeated attacks in the face of withering Union fire, taking heavy casualties and engaging in fierce hand-to-hand combat that continues after nightfall.

7. Cavalry units contest several fords across the Harpeth, with Union forces driving their opponents back across the river to the south side at about 7.00pm.

8. On the Confederates' extreme left flank, a cavalry force led by Brigadier General James R. Chalmers advances to within 60 yards of the Union line, but does not make an assault.

9. Under cover of darkness, Schofield withdraws his men and heads for Nashville, making this technically a Confederate victory, although at a staggering cost.

50

war." The fighting was to be tragically one-sided. Union forces would expend 100 wagon-loads of ammunition in staving off multiple Confederate attacks. Colonel John Q. Lane, a member of Wagner's ill-fated division, counted 11 distinct assaults (part of the problem for the rebels was the piecemeal nature of their attacks), all of which were repulsed, with savage hand-to-hand fighting along parts of the line. Many Confederate troops found themselves pinned in front of the Union breastworks, unable to advance or retreat. Long after dark the fighting continued, but Schofield's men held and they inflicted staggering losses on Hood's men. The Army of Tennessee suffered an estimated 7,000 casualties, with more than 1,700 killed, although accurate figures are unknown because no official count was taken. Among the dead were Cleburne and five other generals. Union losses amounted to 2,326, with the brunt of these borne by Wagner's men, who suffered 571 casualties and a further 670 missing, presumed captured. Wagner asked to be relieved of command following Franklin and was replaced by Brigadier General Washington L. Elliott.

Schofield was urged by some of his officers to launch a counterattack the following day, but he stuck to his original plan of withdrawing his men to Nashville. Hood, remarkably, put plans in place for a second full-scale assault the next day, and had Schofield stood his ground he may well have broken the Army of Tennessee. As it was, the attempt to prevent Union forces from converging on Nashville had failed, but Hood was still not ready to change his strategy.

PREPARATIONS AT NASHVILLE

On December 1 Schofield's force arrived in Nashville, closely followed by Hood's army. The difference in mood cannot be overstated. The Confederates were demoralized, badly clothed, and hungry. Colonel Ellison Capers of the 24th South Carolina Infantry reported that daily rations sometimes consisted of three ears of corn per man. They also bore resentment for the way they had been used at Franklin and had, to some extent, lost faith in their commanding officer. Brigadier General James A. Smith took command of Cleburne's Division after Franklin and said of the unit's mood: "nor was the tone and morale such as was desirable, owing to the fearful loss sustained in that battle."

In contrast, the Union troops were hugely relieved to have found the sanctuary of the lines around Nashville. They joined the men of XVI Corps, who had started arriving the previous day, and their numbers would soon be swollen further by the arrival of Steedman's Provisional Detachment. The massed ranks of Union soldiers had now reached a formidable number. Based on official returns of December 10, the Union forces at Nashville, present for duty and equipped, were comprised as follows: IV Corps – 14,172; XXIII Corps – 10,207; XVI Corps – 10,280; Provisional Detachment (District of the Etowah) – 7,750; Post of Nashville – 2,027; Cavalry Corps – 11,982. This total of 56,418 men dwarfed Hood's force, which now numbered around 25,000.

Hood was in no condition to attack, and even if his army had been a numerical match for Thomas's, Nashville's defenses were extensive. A line of fortifications stretched for 10 miles, punctuated by forts and

Emerson Opdycke made a habit of timely interventions. It was his brigade that reached Spring Hill in time to repulse Forrest's troopers. Now, at Franklin, his men would plug the gap opened in the Union line. They were only able to do so because Opdycke had apparently refused to align his men with the rest of Wagner's brigade in front of the defensive works. (LOC, LC-B813-1965A)

The Confederate casualty list from the Battle of Franklin was shocking, including the deaths of no fewer than six generals. Among their number was the highly capable Patrick Ronayne Cleburne, an Irishman by birth whose progress in the Confederate Army had been stifled by controversy over his assertion that the slaves should be armed to fight for the South. (LOC, LC-USZ62-12995)

Preparations for Hood's arrival in Nashville. The majestic State Capitol had long been fortified (note the covered guns), but a formidable line of defensive works made it very unlikely that an enemy force would ever reach this far into the city. (LOC, LC-B811- 2629)

blockhouses. The ground to the front of the lines had been cleared of trees to make artillery fire more effective and there was even a second line of entrenchments in case the first was pierced.

Hood settled his men into the hills to the south of the city, their line looking fragile in comparison. Hood's plan was to resist a Union assault and then counterattack, but this was extremely wishful thinking. Many of his men were without shoes and the weather was about to worsen. Deserters were trickling away, but there was little Hood could do but sit and wait. Retreat was not a word in his vocabulary.

The Confederate position seemed hopeless and invited envelopment on one or both flanks, but the anticipated attack did not come. Thomas wanted an effective cavalry force and he was short of horses. Nashville was scoured for suitable mounts, while Thomas was bombarded with telegrams from Grant, urging him to attack. Thomas' reputation as "the Rock of Chickamauga" now worked against him. There was concern that he was capable only of stubborn defense, and the delay in attacking a clearly inferior enemy seemed to confirm this.

On December 7 Grant delivered as clear an order as possible: "Attack Hood at once and await no longer the remount of your cavalry." Grant's concern was partially justified. Too many times over the course of the war Union forces had failed to deliver a decisive blow when all seemed in place. If Hood was to escape now his army could recover and continue to pose a threat. Yet Grant, at a distance, could not appreciate the situation at Nashville. Hood's battered army was making no threatening moves

A Colored Battery assembles in Tennessee. Two Colored Brigades fought at Nashville as part of Steedman's Provisional Detachment, while Battery A of the 2nd US Colored Artillery helped man the defensive lines. (LOC, LC-B811-2646)

and appeared content to sit and wait. Thomas probably felt there was no need to hurry and wanted to make his preparations exactly right. He made plans to attack on December 10, but the day before a severe winter storm made operations impossible. Ice lay up to an inch thick on the ground, bringing misery to both sets of troops, although the Federal forces at least had sufficient supplies. More trees were chopped down to make campfires and evidence suggests that the Confederates built fires at 6ft intervals along their lines in a desperate attempt to keep warm.

Efforts were also made to solidify the Confederate position, with five redoubts constructed to anchor the extreme left of the line. Each was intended to house a four-gun battery, with infantry support. The right of the line was positioned adjacent to a deep railroad cutting, providing protection. Granbury's Brigade, of Cleburne's Division, was ordered to construct a lunette capable of holding 300 men to further strengthen the right flank. The Confederate line also covered four roads, offering a line of retreat if absolutely necessary.

Cheatham's Corps was positioned on the right, with Stewart's on the left. This meant that the two corps that had suffered most at Franklin were holding the flanks. Lee's Corps, which had mostly missed out at Franklin, was positioned in the center of the line. A single cavalry division, under Brigadier General James R. Chalmers, was posted to cover the 4-mile gap between the Confederate left flank and the Cumberland, an impossibly large expanse. On December 10 Hood weakened this force still further, ordering the brigade of Colonel Jacob B. Biffle to the right flank. Chalmers voiced his concerns and was provided a single brigade of infantry, Ector's Brigade, now under the command of Colonel David Coleman and numbering a paltry 700 after the ravages of Franklin.

53

Chalmers' division comprised the entirety of Hood's cavalry forces, because on December 7 he had made a serious tactical error. The bulk of Forrest's cavalry and a 1,600-strong infantry force under Major General William B. Bate had been dispatched to Murfreesborough to confront Union forces there. The operation proved fruitless and Bate rejoined Hood on December 9, but Forrest did not. It is uncertain whether Hood hoped to draw Union forces away from Nashville, but if that was indeed his aim more suitable bait could have been found than two divisions of Forrest's tough troopers, who would be badly missed. As the weather improved on December 13 it became clear that the long-awaited confrontation was nearing. Hood attempted to recall Forrest but did not get a message to him in time.

Thomas issued Special Orders No. 342, outlining the plans for the assault. Although simple in essence, they involved a great deal of maneuvering to get into position. Steedman's Provisional Detachment was to move out of the Nashville lines along the Murfreesborough Turnpike and make an assault on the extreme right of the Confederate line. This was intended to be a pinning move, while the main attack focused on the left. IV Corps (now led by Wood following a wound sustained by Stanley at Franklin) and Smith's XVI Corps were to move out of their positions and wheel to the left. They would smash into the left of the Confederate line, precisely where Hood had placed his redoubts. Schofield's XXIII Corps was to undertake a lengthy march from the Union left to its right, taking up a position behind Wood and

Smith to act as a reserve. Finally, Wilson's cavalry was to push out along the Charlotte Pike, before dividing, with units joining the great left wheel of the bulk of the Union forces. Hood's center would be unmolested under this plan, meaning that his freshest troops would be relegated to the role of bystanders.

THE BATTLE OF NASHVILLE – THE FIRST DAY

At 4.00am on December 15 reveille was sounded and the troops awakened to a fog-bound battlefield that was to make movement awkward and slow. Partly because of this, and partly because of the elaborate nature of the Union maneuvers themselves, it was hours before action commenced.

On the Union left, Steedman's men began to move out at 6.00am. At 9.00am they launched their diversionary assault on the Confederate right wing. Three regiments of US Colored Troops under Colonel Thomas J. Morgan skirted Granbury's lunette, but were caught in a crossfire and forced to retire with heavy losses. Lieutenant Colonel Charles Grosvenor's 3rd Brigade was also easily repulsed by the men of Granbury's Brigade, led by Captain Edward T. Broughton. A second attack would be launched by Steedman's soldiers at 11.00am, but they never tested the Confederate defenses. The diversion was also insufficient to fool Hood into thinking a major assault was taking place. He called no reinforcements from his center, but Steedman's efforts did at least pin the Confederate right, and that was its main purpose.

The real work was taking place to the west. Wood's IV Corps had been ready to move at 6.00am, but fog and deep mud had made maneuvering difficult. By 7.30am his men had left their lines and taken up their preliminary positions for the assault. Each of the three divisions prepared to advance with a two-brigade front, the third brigades kept as reserves, but they would wait a while yet. Schofield's shift of position was taking a long time and Smith's XVI Corps was obstructing Wilson's cavalry. At 10.00am, Wilson and Smith moved. The huge, swinging door of the Union advance was set in motion, pivoting on Wood's corps, which could do nothing but wait, with the stretched Confederate left flank as the target.

Wilson's formidable cavalry brushed aside Chalmers' small force of 900 troopers and sent Ector's Brigade hurrying back to the Confederate lines, as ordered, where they took up position on the extremity of the left flank. Hood, alive to the threat, ordered men from Major General Edward Johnson's Division, in the center of the Confederate line, to reinforce the left. It was a small gesture, but all that Hood could manage with the men at his disposal. The brigades of Deas and Manigault hurried to add what they could to the defense of the left flank.

At 12.30pm, Wood's men were finally ordered to advance. The obstacle in front of them looked formidable, the 150ft-high Montgomery Hill, but the western side of the hill offered a shallower slope than the front face. The assault would take place there, carried out by Brigadier General Samuel Beatty's 3rd Division. At 1.00pm, the Second Brigade advanced, in Wood's words, "as sweeps the stiff gale over the ocean." With support from the 1st Brigade, the hill was soon in Union hands, and only

James B. Steedman's Provisional Detachment, District of the Etowah, would have the honor of making the first assault in the Battle of Nashville. It would be a diversionary movement against the Confederate right flank, intended to hold the rebels in position while the real work was done on the other side of the battlefield. (LOC, LC-B813-2024A)

then was it realized that this position had been abandoned by all but a line of skirmishers. The main Confederate line was more than half a mile distant and heavily manned. Wood's work was far from done.

Elsewhere, the smooth Union plan was running into difficulties. The Union line was not extending as far to the southwest as Thomas had intended, and there was danger that the movement would not outflank the Confederates. With the luxury of his vastly superior manpower Thomas was able, at 1.00pm, to simply call Schofield into the line to extend it. Wood's reserve brigades were also called forward, to fill a gap between his men and those of Smith's XVI Corps. This simple but effective use of reserve troops contrasts painfully with the limited options at Hood's disposal.

On the Confederate left Stewart was well aware that he was facing the brunt of the Union assault. He called up Major General Edward C. Walthall's reserve division and ordered him to place 100 men in each of redoubts No. 4 and No. 5, as well as two guns in No. 5 (No. 4 already having a complement of four guns). The bulk of Walthall's division was then to be positioned behind a stone wall that ran roughly parallel with the line of redoubts, starting around No. 3 and ending behind No. 4. This line was to have no artillery support. Apart from the guns placed in the redoubts, the remainder of Walthall's artillery had been dispersed along the main line.

As the Union forces left their positions at Nashville on a fog-bound morning, the defensive line was left in the hands of the garrison troops. The tents visible here would no doubt have been very welcome during the bitterly cold weather leading up to the battle. (LOC, LC-B813-2024A)

Another view from the Union defensive line on the first day of the Battle of Nashville. Note the absence of trees in front of the line. On the hill to the right of the picture sits the blockhouse Casino. (LOC, LC-B811-2640)

The incomplete redoubt No. 5 was isolated, and was to be the first to feel the weight of the Union advance. Dismounted cavalry from Brigadier General Edward Hatch's 5th Division swarmed over the lightly defended fort, instantly turning the guns so recently placed there by Walthall on the men in redoubt No. 4, where Captain Charles L. Lumsden put up stubborn resistance with his 100 infantrymen of the 29th Alabama and four guns. Overwhelming opposition would force him to abandon the position, but only after his gunners had fled with the friction primers necessary to fire the guns.

Redoubt No. 3 now received attention from the men of Colonel Sylvester G. Hill's 3rd Brigade, 1st Division, XVI Corps. A full-blooded charge saw the redoubt taken, but as Hill ordered his men to continue to redoubt No. 2 he died from a shot to the head. The charge continued, however, and the next redoubt was taken. Stewart's flank was now held by the few brigades posted behind the stone wall and the more formidable redoubt No. 1. With Wilson's cavalry lapping around the open end of his line, his position was rapidly becoming untenable. During the Union assaults on the redoubts, Ector's Brigade had become detached from the left of Walthall's Division. Walthall did his best to compensate, moving Reynolds' Brigade (Brigadier General Daniel H. Reynolds) from the right of his line to the left and filling the void by stretching the other two brigades even more thinly. The need for reinforcements was acute, but

EVENTS

1. Before dawn, Schofield's XXIII Corps moves from its position in the lines around Nashville to take part in the planned assault on the Confederate left flank.

2. Around 6am the siege guns of Fort Negley open fire.

3. At 6am, under cover of a heavy fog, Steedman's Provisional Detachment, District of the Etowah, advances down Murfreesborough Pike to stage a diversionary attack on the Confederate right flank.

4. 8AM: Steedman's men, including the 1st and 2nd US Colored Troops Brigades, attack and are easily repulsed. Thompson's 2nd USCT Brigade occupies some abandoned works and does not move for the rest of the day.

5. 10AM: Wilson's Cavalry Division moves out along Charlotte Pike, driving Rucker's Brigade away and forcing Ector's Brigade of infantry to fall back to the main Confederate lines.

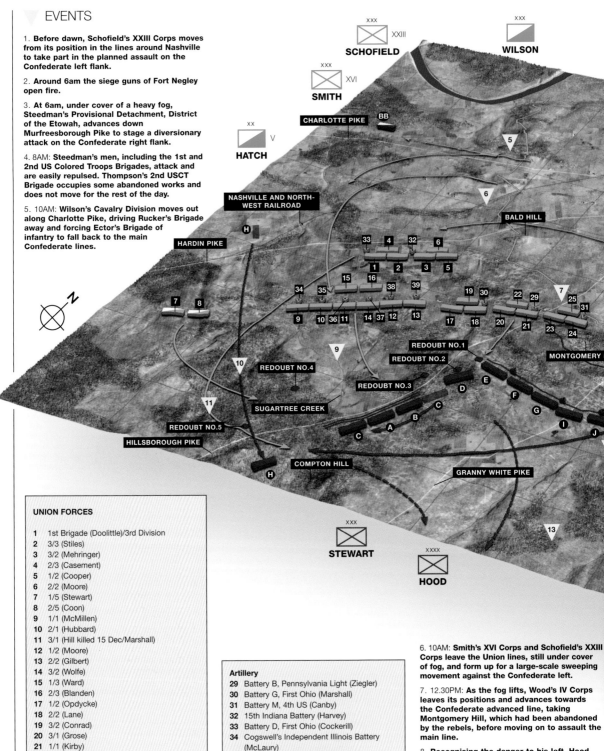

UNION FORCES

1	1st Brigade (Doolittle)/3rd Division
2	3/3 (Stiles)
3	3/2 (Mehringer)
4	2/3 (Casement)
5	1/2 (Cooper)
6	2/2 (Moore)
7	1/5 (Stewart)
8	2/5 (Coon)
9	1/1 (McMillen)
10	2/1 (Hubbard)
11	3/1 (Hill killed 15 Dec/Marshall)
12	1/2 (Moore)
13	2/2 (Gilbert)
14	3/2 (Wolfe)
15	1/3 (Ward)
16	2/3 (Blanden)
17	1/2 (Opdycke)
18	2/2 (Lane)
19	3/2 (Conrad)
20	3/1 (Grose)
21	1/1 (Kirby)
22	2/1 (Wittaker)
23	2/3 (Post)
24	1/3 (Streight)
25	3/3 (Knefler)
26	2nd USCT Brigade (Thompson)
27	3rd Brigade (Grosvenor)/Cruft's Division
28	1st USCT Brigade (Morgan)

Artillery

29	Battery B, Pennsylvania Light (Ziegler)
30	Battery G, First Ohio (Marshall)
31	Battery M, 4th US (Canby)
32	15th Indiana Battery (Harvey)
33	Battery D, First Ohio (Cockerill)
34	Cogswell's Independent Illinois Battery (McLaury)
35	Second Iowa Battery (Reed)
36	Battery I, Second Missouri (Julian)
37	Battery G, Second Illinois (Lowell)
38	Ninth Indiana Battery (Calfee)
39	Third Indiana Battery (Ginn)
40	20th Indiana Battery (Osborne)
41	18th Ohio Battery (Aleshire)

6. 10AM: Smith's XVI Corps and Schofield's XXIII Corps leave the Union lines, still under cover of fog, and form up for a large-scale sweeping movement against the Confederate left.

7. 12.30PM: As the fog lifts, Wood's IV Corps leaves its positions and advances towards the Confederate advanced line, taking Montgomery Hill, which had been abandoned by the rebels, before moving on to assault the main line.

8. Recognising the danger to his left, Hood moves elements of Johnson's Division from their central position to the left.

9. 1PM: Smith's Division hits Confederate Redoubt No.4, which holds out for around three hours before the 100 men of the 29th Alabama and 48 artillerymen are forced to retreat in the face of overwhelming Union strength.

BATTLE OF NASHVILLE – DAY ONE, DECEMBER 15, 1864

After a spell of bitterly cold weather, December 14 saw temperatures rise enough to thaw the ground around Nashville. At dawn on December 15, Thomas' army moved out from its lines in overwhelming numbers to confront Hood's Army of Tennessee, concentrating on the Confederates' left flank while pinning the right with a diversionary assault.

Note: Gridlines are shown at intervals of 1km (1093yds)

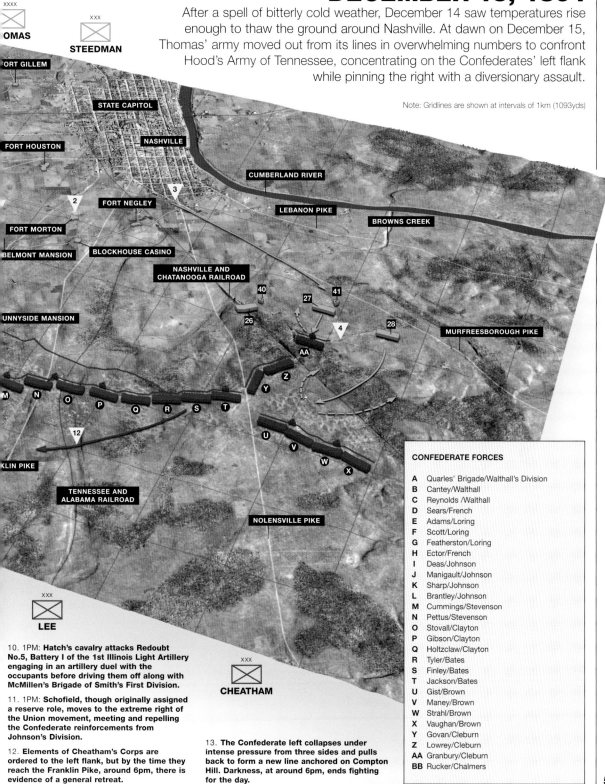

10. 1PM: **Hatch's cavalry attacks Redoubt No.5, Battery I of the 1st Illinois Light Artillery engaging in an artillery duel with the occupants before driving them off along with McMillen's Brigade of Smith's First Division.**

11. 1PM: **Schofield, though originally assigned a reserve role, moves to the extreme right of the Union movement, meeting and repelling the Confederate reinforcements from Johnson's Division.**

12. **Elements of Cheatham's Corps are ordered to the left flank, but by the time they reach the Franklin Pike, around 6pm, there is evidence of a general retreat.**

13. **The Confederate left collapses under intense pressure from three sides and pulls back to form a new line anchored on Compton Hill. Darkness, at around 6pm, ends fighting for the day.**

CONFEDERATE FORCES

A	Quarles' Brigade/Walthall's Division
B	Cantey/Walthall
C	Reynolds /Walthall
D	Sears/French
E	Adams/Loring
F	Scott/Loring
G	Featherston/Loring
H	Ector/French
I	Deas/Johnson
J	Manigault/Johnson
K	Sharp/Johnson
L	Brantley/Johnson
M	Cummings/Stevenson
N	Pettus/Stevenson
O	Stovall/Clayton
P	Gibson/Clayton
Q	Holtzclaw/Clayton
R	Tyler/Bates
S	Finley/Bates
T	Jackson/Bates
U	Gist/Brown
V	Maney/Brown
W	Strahl/Brown
X	Vaughan/Brown
Y	Govan/Cleburn
Z	Lowrey/Cleburn
AA	Granbury/Cleburn
BB	Rucker/Chalmers

Nathan Kimball's 1st Division would spearhead the assault against the main Confederate line on the first day of the Battle of Nashville, triggering the collapse of the Confederate left flank and the withdrawal to a second line.
(LOC, LC-B813-1647B)

when the brigades of Deas and Manigault arrived they were almost instantly driven back, "making but feeble resistance" in Stewart's words. The situation was becoming increasingly perilous as Federal troops moved in force past the exposed flank.

Wood's IV Corps, having waited patiently after taking the lightly defended Montgomery Hill, was now ordered to assault the main line. Brigadier General Nathan Kimball's 1st Division was selected to attack, with support from Elliott's 2nd Division. A half-hour bombardment by Union artillery softened up the Confederate position, then Kimball's men began to move through a heavy, muddy cornfield, before tackling fallen timber and heavy brush on the slope up to the redoubt. The men of the 80th Illinois, 84th Illinois, and 9th Indiana were at the forefront of the attack. Colonel Isaac Suman of the 9th Indiana commented that the going was so slow that, about 60 paces from the Confederate line, he ordered his men to stop, remove their knapsacks and then continue. The three spearhead regiments suffered a combined total of just two fatalities and the strongest redoubt in the Confederate defenses had fallen.

The men in Stewart's line can hardly be blamed for yielding. Under attack from two sides, with Union forces also pressing into the rear as Walthall's men were pushed back from their wall, the position was hopeless. Stewart ordered his men to withdraw. Reinforcements from Cheatham's Corps (Bate's Division) crossed the Granny White Turnpike as the tattered left flank was withdrawing. "When I passed the Franklin turnpike," Bate would write, "streams of stragglers, and artillerists, and horses, without guns or caissons, the sure indicia of defeat, came hurriedly from the left." Attempting to stem the Union tide, Bate's men were driven back by Schofield's XXIII Corps in its first action of the day.

The remainder of the day would be a confused affair, as Confederate officers pulled their commands together and assumed a new defensive position about 2 miles back from the original line. Darkness fell at around 6.00pm and Union troops bivouacked for the night, unsure of whether there would be an opponent to fight again the next day.

THE BATTLE OF NASHVILLE – THE SECOND DAY

Whether the uncertainty spread to the upper echelons or not, there appears to have been some confusion among the Union ranks. There is no record of any official orders disseminated by Thomas, although in official reports many officers refer to acting upon orders. Certainly the Union effort of the second day of the Battle of Nashville was less coordinated. Hood had drawn his men into a tighter line that presented a formidable obstacle. Stewart's shaken corps was placed at the center of the new line, with Cheatham's relatively fresh men moved to the left flank and Lee's Corps taking the right. At both ends of the 2-mile line, commanding hills offered naturally strong positions, but the line was short and vulnerable to outflanking. Equally worrying for the Confederates, they now covered only two potential lines of retreat, the Granny White and Franklin turnpikes.

For much of the morning of December 16 the Union forces moved into position to continue the offensive as a cold rain fell. Steedman again took the extreme left flank, joined in order by Wood, Smith, and Schofield. Wilson's cavalry was to take the extreme right of the line, as it had the day before, but this time it curved around the Confederate positions, with Cheatham's Corps doubling back on itself in an effort to stave off what would be a disastrous outflanking.

On the Confederate right, Lee's men would face a sterner challenge than Cheatham's Corps had in the same position the previous day. Wood's men had approached the Confederate skirmishers and, although held up by a stream 50 yards in front of the rebels, had succeeded in driving them back to the main line. An artillery duel followed that delighted Wood ("It was really entertaining to witness it."), during which Thomas visited to request a demonstration on the Confederate right flank. Wood was also to be alert to any opportunity to make a more determined attack.

Colonel Sidney Post was ordered to reconnoiter the position and on his report Wood authorized an assault. At 3.00pm Post's 2nd Brigade advanced, with Steedman's troops joining to his left and further support from Colonel Abel D. Streight's 1st Brigade. Rebel resistance was fierce, with canister and shot from 28 guns well-sited by Lee taking a heavy toll until the advance faltered and men lay down to avoid the destructive fire. Union artillery opened up again, giving fresh impetus to the offensive, but it stalled once more when a line of reserve troops rose amid the Confederate ranks and fired a devastating short-range volley. Post fell, seriously wounded, and momentum was lost. Union soldiers now withdrew in the face of a withering fire, described as "whole sheets of blue liquid lead" by one soldier caught up in the carnage. The Federals had taken 1,000 casualties.

Just as on the previous day, the battle was going better for Thomas on his right. Anchored on the imposing Compton Hill, the left of the Confederate line looked strong, but was fatally flawed. The hill had originally been manned by Ector's Brigade who, though exhausted, had labored through the night to construct defensive works. It was only in the morning that a terrible error was discovered – the breastworks had been constructed too far back from the crest of the hill. Any attacking troops would be sheltered by the steep slope of the hill and would only come under fire over the last few yards of their charge. Worse still, as Bate's men discovered when they took over the position, "The works were flimsy, only intended to protect against small arms, and had no abatis or other obstruction to impede the movements of an assaulting party."

There was no time to do anything to rectify the situation. Bate's division was pinned by accurate and sustained fire from Union artillery and sharpshooters, while to their rear Wilson's troopers, armed with repeating Spencer carbines, were tightening the noose. Sensing disaster, Bate ordered his artillery battalion to retire to the Franklin Turnpike, the Granny White Turnpike having already been closed as an escape route by the advancing Federals. Wilson, seeing the same situation as Bate, though obviously with different emotions, became incensed that Thomas did not launch a concerted infantry assault. He sent rider after rider to suggest a full-scale attack, but the Union forces seemed temporarily

The freedom afforded the Union cavalry by the absence of Forrest's troopers proved especially telling on the second day of the Battle of Nashville, when cavalry forces, including the 7th Division under Joseph F. Knipe (seen here), got behind Cheatham's Corps and fatally undermined the Confederate left wing. (LC, LC-B813-1502 B)

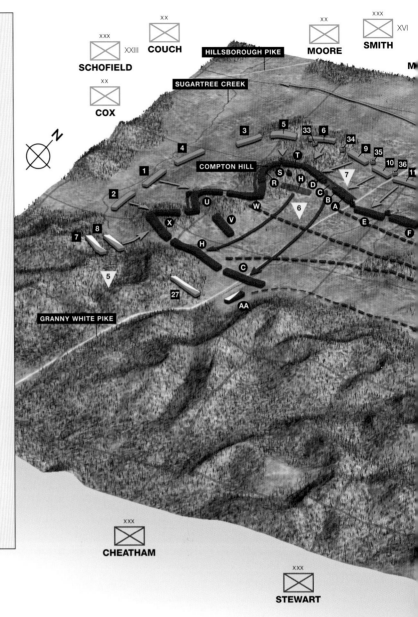

UNION FORCES

1	1st Brigade (Doolittle)/3rd Division
2	3/3 (Stiles)
3	3/2 (Mehringer)
4	2/3 (Casement)
5	1/2 (Cooper)
6	2/2 (Moore)
7	1/5 (Stewart)
8	2/5 (Coon)
9	1/1 (McMillen)
10	2/1 (Hubbard)
11	3/1 (Hill killed 15 Dec/Marshall)
12	1/2 (Moore)
13	2/2 (Gilbert)
14	3/2 (Wolfe)
15	1/2 (Opdycke)
16	2/2 (Lane)
17	3/2 (Conrad)
18	3/1 (Grose)
19	1/1 (Kirby)
20	2/1 (Wittaker)
21	2/3 (Post)
22	1/3 (Streight)
23	2/3 (Knefler)
24	2nd USCT Brigade (Thompson)
25	3rd Brigade (Grosvenor)/Cruft's Division
26	1st USCT Brigade (Morgan)
27	1/7 (Knipe)

Artillery

28	Battery B, Pennsylvania Light (Ziegler)
29	Battery G, First Ohio (Marshall)
30	Battery M, 4th US (Canby)
31	Sixth Ohio Battery (Baldwin)
32	First Kentucky Battery (Thomasson)
33	15th Indiana Battery (Harvey)
34	Cogswell's Independent Illinois Battery (McLaury)
35	Second Iowa Battery (Reed)
36	Battery I, Second Missouri (Julian)
37	Battery G, Second Illinois (Lowell)
38	Ninth Indiana Battery (Calfee)
39	Third Indiana Battery (Ginn)
40	20th Indiana Battery (Osborne)
41	18th Ohio Battery (Aleshire)

▼ EVENTS

1. **Hood withdraws his army to a new defensive position under cover of darkness. Though more compact, it is anchored on imposing hills. However, his forces now only cover two potential avenues of retreat.**

2. **The Union effort is less organised than on the previous day. Most of the morning is taken up getting into position in front of Hood's line.**

3. 2PM: **Anticipating an assault on his right, Hood calls for Cleburne's Division (commanded by James A. Smith following Franklin) to report to him. One brigade (Govan's) is immediately sent back to the left to extend the line, but Lowrey's and Granbury's Brigades move to reinforce Lee.**

4. 3PM: **Once more it is the left of the Union line that sees the first action, but rebel resistance is fierce, inflicting 1,000 casualties on the attacking forces.**

5. 3PM: **Federal cavalry have got behind the Confederate line and are putting immense pressure on Cheatham's Corps.**

6. 3PM: **Cheatham thins his line by sending troops to cover his rear, but the Union forces close in inexorably, cutting off the Granny White Pike as a potential line of retreat.**

7. 4PM: **After long delay, the main Union assault on Compton Hill begins. Stubborn resistance from the rebel defenders cannot prevent their position from being overrun.**

8. **The Army of Tennessee collapses from the left and is soon in headlong retreat down the only road still open to them, the Franklin Pike.**

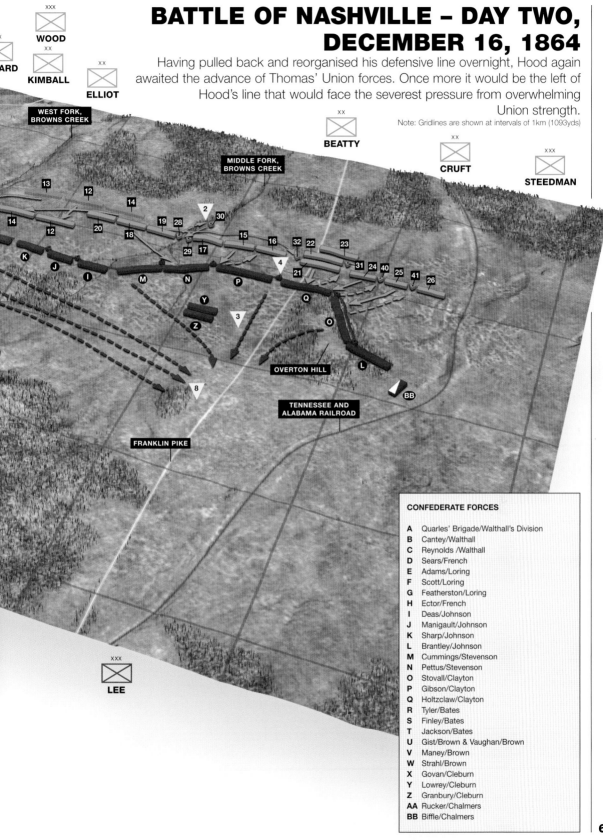

BATTLE OF NASHVILLE – DAY TWO, DECEMBER 16, 1864

Having pulled back and reorganised his defensive line overnight, Hood again awaited the advance of Thomas' Union forces. Once more it would be the left of Hood's line that would face the severest pressure from overwhelming Union strength.

Note: Gridlines are shown at intervals of 1km (1093yds)

WOOD

RD

KIMBALL

ELLIOT

WEST FORK, BROWNS CREEK

MIDDLE FORK, BROWNS CREEK

BEATTY

CRUFT

STEEDMAN

OVERTON HILL

TENNESSEE AND ALABAMA RAILROAD

FRANKLIN PIKE

LEE

CONFEDERATE FORCES

A	Quarles' Brigade/Walthall's Division
B	Cantey/Walthall
C	Reynolds /Walthall
D	Sears/French
E	Adams/Loring
F	Scott/Loring
G	Featherston/Loring
H	Ector/French
I	Deas/Johnson
J	Manigault/Johnson
K	Sharp/Johnson
L	Brantley/Johnson
M	Cummings/Stevenson
N	Pettus/Stevenson
O	Stovall/Clayton
P	Gibson/Clayton
Q	Holtzclaw/Clayton
R	Tyler/Bates
S	Finley/Bates
T	Jackson/Bates
U	Gist/Brown & Vaughan/Brown
V	Maney/Brown
W	Strahl/Brown
X	Govan/Cleburn
Y	Lowrey/Cleburn
Z	Granbury/Cleburn
AA	Rucker/Chalmers
BB	Biffle/Chalmers

paralyzed. As the day wore on and no attack came, it even became possible that no decisive move would be made before nightfall.

Although opinions vary on the cause for the delay, there is much evidence that Schofield was reluctant to order his men forward, fearing the Confederate position was too strong. While he was standing with Thomas and surveying the lines, the day began to drift away and some units were actually given orders to bivouac for the night. To Schofield's left, Smith's corps also waited with some impatience. General John McArthur, commanding the 1st Division, took matters into his own hands, sending Thomas a message that he was about to attack unless he received orders to the contrary. He received no such orders and, at around 4.00pm, ordered his men forward against Compton Hill.

A day that had been slipping toward an inconclusive end now changed shape dramatically. Thomas ordered Schofield to join the advance and the men storming Compton Hill found to their delight that they were sheltered from the rebel guns by the misplacement of the defensive works. Bate's men resisted and suffered heavy casualties, among them Lieutenant Colonel William M. Shy (after whom the hill is now named), but the odds were overwhelming. On the left of the Union forces, Wood suddenly heard a great shout rise up from thousands of throats and knew what it meant. Ordering his corps forward en masse, he watched his men sweep over the rebel lines at all points. "Military history scarcely affords a parallel of a more complete victory," he would later write.

The Army of Tennessee collapsed from the left, the rout spreading down the line and infecting those facing Wood's corps, despite the fact that they had beaten back a determined assault earlier in the day. Official battle reports from Union commanders repeat a common theme – they took almost no losses in the final assault because the rebel troops either aimed too high or simply fled, all cohesion gone. Though it would rally sufficiently to stage a fighting withdrawal over the coming days, the Army of Tennessee had effectively ceased to exist. It never went into battle again.

Blame for the destruction of an army has inevitably been lain at the feet of Hood, whose leadership was little more than a succession of errors, each seemingly more serious than the last. Standing and fighting against Thomas' overwhelming forces at Nashville may have been the biggest, although Sherman is not the only observer to have gone on record as saying that the Battle of Nashville was won at Franklin.

Thomas was vindicated in the eyes of his superiors, and lauded for the most decisive victory of the entire war, but in truth it would have been remarkable had he not utterly crushed Hood's battered army. The Confederate retreat took place in terrible weather, with a rotating rearguard staving off Union pursuers and the tattered ranks of rebels leaving bloody footprints on the frozen ground. The arrival of Forrest's troopers, on December 19, gave them an effective response to the probing Union cavalrymen, but it is impossible not to wonder what they might have been able to do four days earlier. On December 26, Hood's exhausted army began crossing the Tennessee River and the Union pursuit was called off three days later. On reaching Tupelo, Mississippi, in January 1865, Hood's army was found to number scarcely 20,000, meaning he had lost half the men with which he had crossed into Tennessee at the start of his campaign.

Hood's official report, of February 15, 1865, remained defiant:

At Nashville, had it not been for an unfortunate event [he did not elaborate on this enigmatic statement] *which could not justly have been anticipated, I think we would have gained a complete victory. It is my firm conviction that, not withstanding that disaster, I left the army in better spirits and with more confidence in itself than it had in the opening of the campaign. Were I again placed in such circumstances I should make the same marches and fight the same battles, trusting that the same unforeseen and unavoidable accident would not again occur to change into disaster a victory which had been already won.*

Beauregard was far less impressed with Hood's tenure at the head of the Army of Tennessee, commenting that "It is clear ... to my mind that after the great loss and waste of life at Franklin, the army was in no condition to make a successful attack on Nashville." Beauregard also took pains to praise Hood's men in his report of April 15, 1865:

The heroic dead of that campaign will ever be recollected with honor by their countrymen, and the survivors have the proud consolation that no share of the disaster can be laid to them, who have so worthily served their country, and have stood by their colors even to the last dark hours of the republic.

There was no time to wallow in sentiment immediately after Nashville, however. In Georgia, Sherman was nearing his goal.

ORDERS OF BATTLE

THE BATTLE OF NASHVILLE, DECEMBER 15–16, 1864

UNION FORCES
Overall command:
   Major General George H. Thomas

IV Corps
Brigadier General Thomas J. Wood
(14,172 men)

1st Division
Brigadier General Nathan Kimball

1st Brigade –
   Colonel Isaac M. Kirby
21st Illinois
38th Illinois
31st Indiana
81st Indiana
90th Ohio
101st Ohio

2nd Brigade –
   Brigadier General Walter C. Whitaker
96th Illinois
115th Illinois
35th Indiana
21st Kentucky
23rd Kentucky
45th Ohio
51st Ohio

3rd Brigade –
   Brigadier General William Grose
75th Illinois
80th Illinois
84th Illinois
9th Indiana
30th Indiana
36th Indiana (one company)
84th Indiana
77th Pennsylvania

2nd Division
Brigadier General Washington L. Elliott

1st Brigade – Colonel Emerson Opdycke
36th Illinois
44th Illinois
73rd Illinois
74th Illinois
88th Illinois
125th Ohio
24th Wisconsin

2nd Brigade – Colonel John Q. Lane
100th Illinois
40th Indiana
57th Indiana
28th Kentucky
26th Ohio
97th Ohio

3rd Brigade – Colonel Joseph Conrad
42nd Illinois
51st Illinois
79th Illinois

15th Missouri
64th Ohio
65th Ohio

3rd Division
Brigadier General Samuel Beatty

1st Brigade – Colonel Abel D. Streight
89th Illinois
51st Indiana
8th Kansas
15th Ohio
49th Ohio

2nd Brigade – Colonel Sidney Post
59th Illinois
41st Ohio
71st Ohio
93rd Ohio
124th Ohio

3rd Brigade – Colonel Frederick Knefler
79th Indiana
86th Indiana
13th Ohio
19th Ohio

Artillery
Major William F. Godspeed

Indiana Light, 25th Battery
Kentucky Light, 1st Battery
1st Michigan Light, Battery E
1st Ohio Light, Battery G
Ohio Light, 6th Battery
Pennsylvania Light, Battery B
4th United States, Battery M

XXIII Corps
Major General John M. Schofield
(10,207 men)

2nd Division
Major General Darius N. Couch

1st Brigade –
   Brigadier General Joseph A. Cooper
130th Indiana
26th Kentucky
25th Michigan
99th Ohio
3rd Tennessee
6th Tennessee

2nd Brigade – Colonel Orlando H. Moore
107th Illinois
80th Indiana
129th Indiana
23rd Michigan
111th Ohio
118th Ohio

3rd Brigade – Colonel John Mehringer
91st Indiana

123rd Indiana
50th Ohio
183rd Ohio

Artillery
Indiana Light, 15th Battery
Ohio Light, 19th Battery

3rd Division
Brigadier General Jacob D. Cox

1st Brigade – Colonel Charles C. Doolittle
12th Kentucky
16th Kentucky
100th Ohio
104th Ohio
8th Tennessee

2nd Brigade – Colonel John S. Casement
65th Illinois
65th Indiana
124th Indiana
103rd Ohio
5th Tennessee

3rd Brigade – Colonel Israel N. Stiles
112th Illinois
63rd Indiana
120th Indiana
128th Indiana

Artillery
Indiana Light, 23rd Battery
1st Ohio Light, Battery D

XVI Corps – Detachment Army of the Tennessee
Major General Andrew J. Smith
(10,280 men)

1st Division
Brigadier General John McArthur

1st Brigade – Colonel William L. McMillen
114th Illinois
93rd Indiana
10th Minnesota
72nd Ohio
95th Ohio
Illinois Light Artillery, Cogswell's Battery

2nd Brigade – Colonel Lucius F. Hubbard
5th Minnesota
9th Minnesota
11th Missouri
8th Wisconsin
Iowa Light Artillery, 2nd Battery

3rd Brigade – Colonel Sylvester G. Hill/
   Colonel William R. Marshall
12th Iowa
35th Iowa
7th Minnesota

33rd Missouri
2nd Missouri Light Artillery, Battery I

2nd Division
Brigadier General Kenner Garrard

1st Brigade – Colonel David Moore
119th Illinois
122nd Illinois
89th Indiana
21st Missouri
Indiana Light Artillery, 9th Battery

2nd Brigade – Colonel James I. Gilbert
58th Illinois
27th Iowa
32nd Iowa
10th Kansas
Indiana Light Artillery, 3rd Battery

3rd Brigade – Colonel Edward H. Wolfe
49th Illinois
117th Illinois
52nd Indiana
178th New York
2nd Illinois Light Artillery, Battery G

3rd Division
Colonel Jonathan B. Moore

1st Brigade – Colonel Lyman M. Ward
72nd Illinois
40th Missouri
14th Wisconsin
33rd Wisconsin

2nd Brigade – Colonel Leander Blanden
81st Illinois
95th Illinois
44th Missouri

Artillery
Indiana Light, 14th Battery
2nd Missouri Light, Battery A

Provisional Detachment (District of the Etowah)
Major General James B. Steedman
(7,750 men)

Provisional Division
(Composed mainly of detachments
belonging to XIV, XV, XVII, and XX Corps,
which had been unable to rejoin their proper
commands serving with Sherman's army on
the march through Georgia.)
Brigadier General Charles Cruft

1st Brigade – Colonel Benjamin Harrison
Three battalions from XX Corps

2nd Brigade – Colonel John G. Mitchell
Men from detached duty Army of the
Tennessee

*3rd Brigade –
    Lieutenant Colonel Charles H. Grosvenor*
68th Indiana
18th Ohio

*2nd Brigade, Army of the Tennessee –
    Colonel Adam G. Malloy*

Artillery
Indiana Light, 20th Battery
Ohio Light, 18th Battery

*1st Colored Brigade –
    Colonel Thomas J. Morgan*
14th US Colored Troops
16th US Colored Troops
17th US Colored Troops
18th US Colored Troops
44th US Colored Troops

*2nd Colored Brigade –
    Colonel Charles R. Thompson*
12th US Colored Troops
13th US Colored Troops
100th US Colored Troops
Kansas Light Artillery, 1st Battery

Post of Nashville
Brigadier General John F. Miller
(2,027 men)

*2nd Brigade, 4th Division, XX Corps –
    Colonel Edwin C. Mason*
142nd Indiana
45th New York
176th Ohio
179th Ohio
182nd Ohio

Unattached
3rd Kentucky
28th Michigan
173rd Ohio
78th Pennsylvania (detachment)
Veteran Reserve Corps
44th Wisconsin (battalion)
45th Wisconsin (battalion)

Garrison Artillery
Major John J. Ely

Illinois Light, Bridges' Battery
Indiana Light, 2nd Battery
Indiana Light, 4th Battery
Indiana Light, 12th Battery
Indiana Light, 21st Battery
Indiana Light, 22nd Battery
Indiana Light, 24th Battery
1st Michigan Light, Battery F
1st Ohio Light, Battery A
1st Ohio Light, Battery E
Ohio Light, 20th Battery
1st Tennessee Light, Battery C
1st Tennessee Light, Battery D
2nd US Colored Light, Battery A

Quartermaster's Division
Brevet Brigadier General James L. Donaldson

Cavalry Corps
Brevet Major General James H. Wilson
(11,982 men)

Escort
4th United States

1st Division
Brigadier General Edward M. McCook
(absent with 2nd and 3rd Brigades on an
expedition into western Kentucky)

*1st Brigade –
    Brigadier General John T. Croxton*
8th Iowa
4th Kentucky
2nd Michigan

1st Tennessee
Illinois Light Artillery, Board of Trade Battery

5th Division
Brigadier General Edward Hatch

1st Brigade – Colonel Robert R. Stewart
3rd Illinois
11th Indiana
12th Missouri
10th Tennessee

2nd Brigade – Colonel Datus E. Coon
6th Illinois
7th Illinois
9th Illinois
2nd Iowa
12th Tennessee
1st Illinois Light Artillery, Battery I

6th Division
Brigadier General Richard W. Johnson

1st Brigade – Colonel Thomas J. Harrison
16th Illinois
5th Iowa
7th Ohio

2nd Brigade – Colonel James Biddle
14th Illinois
6th Indiana
8th Michigan
3rd Tennessee

Artillery
4th United States, Battery I

7th Division
Brigadier General Joseph F. Knipe

*1st Brigade – Brevet Brigadier General John
    H. Hammond*
9th Illinois
10th Indiana
19th Pennsylvania
2nd Tennessee
4th Tennessee

2nd Brigade – Colonel Gilbert M. L. Johnson
12th Indiana
13th Indiana
6th Tennessee

Artillery
Ohio Light, 14th Battery

CONFEDERATE FORCES

The Army of Tennessee
Overall command: General John Bell Hood
(Approximately 25,000 men)

Lee's Army Corps
Lieutenant General Stephen D. Lee

Johnson's Division
Major General Edward Johnson

*Deas' Brigade –
  Brigadier General Zach C. Deas*
19th Alabama
22nd Alabama
25th Alabama
39th Alabama
50th Alabama

*Manigault's Brigade –
  Lieutenant Colonel William L. Butler*
24th Alabama
28th Alabama
34th Alabama
10th South Carolina
19th South Carolina

*Sharp's Brigade –
  Brigadier General Jacob H. Sharp*
7th & 9th Mississippi
10th & 44th Mississippi
41st Mississippi

*Brantly's Brigade –
  Brigadier General William F. Brantly*
24th & 34th Mississippi
27th Mississippi
29th & 30th Mississippi
Dismounted Cavalry

Stevenson's Division
Major General Carter L. Stevenson

*Cumming's Brigade –
  Colonel Elihu P. Watkins*
34th Georgia
36th Georgia
39th Georgia
56th Georgia

*Pettus' Brigade –
  Brigadier General Edmund W. Pettus*
20th Alabama
23rd Alabama
30th Alabama
31st Alabama
46th Alabama

*Brown's and Reynolds' Brigades –
  Colonel Joseph B. Palmer**
60th North Carolina
3rd & 18th Tennessee
32nd Tennessee
54th Virginia
63rd Virginia
* reported on detached service. Not present
at Battle of Nashville.

Clayton's Division
Major General Henry D. Clayton

*Stovall's Brigade –
  Brigadier Marcellus A. Stovall*
40th Georgia
41st Georgia
42nd Georgia

43rd Georgia
52nd Georgia

*Holtzclaw's Brigade –
  Brigadier General James T. Holtzclaw*
18th Alabama
32nd & 58th Alabama
36th Alabama
38th Alabama

*Gibson's Brigade –
  Brigadier General Randall L. Gibson*
1st Louisiana
4th Louisiana
13th Louisiana
16th Louisiana
19th Louisiana
20th Louisiana
25th Louisiana
30th Louisiana
4th Louisiana Battalion
14th Louisiana Battalion Sharpshooters

Artillery
Major John W. Johnston

*Courtney's Battalion –
  Captain James P. Douglas*
Dent's (Alabama) Battery
Douglas' (Texas) Battery
Garrity's (Alabama) Battery

*Eldridge's Battalion –
  Captain Charles E. Fenner*
Eufaula (Alabama) Battery
Fenner's (Louisiana) Battery
Stanford's (Mississippi) Battery

*Johnston's Battalion –
  Captain John B. Rowan*
Corput's (Georgia) Battery
Marshall's (Tennessee) Battery
Stephens (Georgia) Light Artillery

Stewart's Army Corps
Lieutenant General Alexander P. Stewart

Loring's Division
Major General William W. Loring

*Featherston's Brigade –
  Brigadier Winfield S. Featherston*
1st Mississippi
3rd Mississippi
22nd Mississippi
31st Mississippi
33rd Mississippi
40th Mississippi
1st Mississippi Battalion

Adams' Brigade – Colonel Robert Lowry
6th Mississippi
14th Mississippi
15th Mississippi
20th Mississippi
23rd Mississippi
43rd Mississippi

Scott's Brigade – Colonel John Snodgrass
55th Alabama
57th Alabama
27th, 35th, & 49th Alabama (consolidated)
12th Louisiana

French's Division
Major General Samuel G. French/Brigadier
  General Claudius Sears
(Having been granted a leave of absence,
French's Division was attached to General
Walthall's.)

Ector's Brigade – Colonel David Coleman
29th North Carolina
39th North Carolina
9th Texas
10th Texas Cavalry (dismounted)
14th Texas Cavalry (dismounted)
32nd Texas Cavalry (dismounted)

*Cockrell's Brigade –
  Colonel Peter C. Flournoy**
1st & 4th Missouri
2nd & 6th Missouri
3rd & 5th Missouri
1st Missouri Cavalry
3rd Missouri Battalion Cavalry
* On arrival at Nashville, Cockrell's Brigade
was detached to the mouth of the Duck
River and was not present at the Battle of
Nashville.

*Sears' Brigade –
  Lieutenant Colonel Reuben H. Shotwell*
4th Mississippi
35th Mississippi
36th Mississippi
39th Mississippi
46th Mississippi
7th Mississippi Battalion

Walthall's Division
Major General Edward C. Walthall

*Quarles' Brigade –
  Brigadier General Charles M. Shelley*
17th Alabama
26th Alabama
29th Alabama
37th Mississippi

*Reynolds' Brigade –
  Brigadier General Daniel H. Reynolds*
1st Arkansas Mounted Rifles (dismounted)
2nd Arkansas Mounted Rifles (dismounted)
4th Arkansas
9th Arkansas
25th Arkansas

Artillery
Lieutenant Colonel Samuel C. Williams

*Trueheart's Battalion – commander not
  indicated on original return*
Lumsden's (Alabama) Battery
Selden's (Alabama) Battery
Tarrant's (Alabama) Battery

*Myrick's Battalion – commander not
  indicated on original return*
Bouanchaud's (Louisiana) Battery
Cowan's (Mississippi) Battery
Darden's (Mississippi) Battery

*Storrs' Battalion – commander not indicated
  on original return*
Guibor's (Missouri) Battery
Hoskins' (Mississippi) Battery
Kolb's (Alabama) Battery

Cheatham's Army Corps
Major General Benjamin F. Cheatham

Brown's Division
Brigadier General Mark P. Lowery (Major General John C. Brown wounded at Franklin)

*Gist's Brigade –
    Lieutenant Colonel Zachariah L. Watters*
46th Georgia
65th Georgia & 8th Georgia Battalion
2nd Georgia Battalion Sharpshooters
16th South Carolina
24th South Carolina

Strahl's Brigade – Colonel Andrew J. Kellar
4th, 5th, 31st, 33rd, & 38th Tennessee
19th, 24th, & 41st Tennessee

Maney's Brigade – Colonel Hume R. Feild
4th (P.A.), 6th, 9th, & 50th Tennessee
1st & 27th Tennessee
8th, 16th, & 28th Tennessee

*Vaughan's Brigade –
    Colonel William M. Watkins*
11th & 29th Tennessee
12th & 47th Tennessee
13th, 51st, 52nd, & 154th Tennessee

Cleburne's Division
Brigadier General James A. Smith

*Smith's Brigade –
    Colonel Charles H. Olmstead**
1st Volunteers, Georgia
54th Georgia
57th Georgia
63rd Georgia
* On detached service, did not participate in battles at Franklin or Nashville.

*Govan's Brigade –
    Brigadier General Daniel C. Govan*
1st, 2nd, 5th, 13th, 15th, & 24th Arkansas
6th & 7th Arkansas
8th & 19th Arkansas

*Lowrey's Brigade –
    Brigadier General Mark P. Lowrey*
16th, 33rd, & 45th Alabama
5th Mississippi & 3rd Mississippi Battalion
8th & 32nd Mississippi

*Granbury's Brigade –
    Captain E. T. Broughton*
5th Confederate
35th Tennessee
6th & 15th Texas
7th Texas
10th Texas
17th & 18th Texas Cavalry (dismounted)
24th & 25th Texas Cavalry (dismounted)
Nutt's (Louisiana) Cavalry Company

Bate's Division
Major General William B. Bate

*Tyler's Brigade –
    Brigadier General Thomas B. Smith*
37th Georgia
4th Georgia Battalion Sharpshooters
2nd, 10th, 20th, 30th, & 37th Tennessee

Finley's Brigade – Major Jacob A. Lash
1st & 3rd Florida
6th Florida

7th Florida
1st Florida Cavalry (dismounted) & 4th
    Florida Infantry

*Jackson's Brigade –
    Brigadier General Henry R. Jackson*
1st Georgia Confederate & 66th Georgia
25th Georgia
29th & 30th Georgia
1st Georgia Battalion Sharpshooters

Artillery
Colonel Melancthon Smith

*Hoxton's Battalion – commander not
    indicated on original return*
Perry's (Florida) Battery
Phelan's (Alabama) Battery
Turner's (Mississippi) Battery

*Hotchkiss' Battalion – commander not
    indicated on original return*
Bledsoe's (Missouri) Battery
Goldthwaite's (Alabama) Battery
Key's (Arkansas) Battery

*Cobb's Battalion – commander not indicated
    on original return*
Ferguson's (South Carolina) Battery
Phillips'/Melbane's (Tennessee) Battery
Slocomb's (Louisiana) Battery

Cavalry Corps
Major General Nathan Bedford Forrest

Chalmers' Division
Brigadier General James R. Chalmers

*Rucker's Brigade –
    Colonel Edmund W. Rucker*
7th Alabama
5th Mississippi
7th Tennessee
12th Tennessee
14th Tennessee
15th Tennessee
Forrest's Regiment Tennessee Cavalry

Biffle's Brigade – Colonel Jacob B. Biffle
10th Tennessee

Buford's Division
Brigadier General Abraham Buford
(At Murfreesborough during Battle of Nashville)

Bell's Brigade – Colonel Tyree H. Bell
2nd Tennessee
19th Tennessee
20th Tennessee
21st Tennessee
Nixon's Tennessee Regiment

*Crossland's Brigade –
    Colonel Edward Crossland*
3rd Kentucky Mounted Infantry
7th Kentucky Mounted Infantry
8th Kentucky Mounted Infantry
12th Kentucky Mounted Infantry
12th Kentucky
Huey's Kentucky Battalion

Jackson's Division
Brigadier General William H. Jackson
(At Murfreesborough during Battle of Nashville)

*Armstrong's Brigade –
    Brigadier General Frank C. Armstrong*
1st Mississippi
2nd Mississippi
28th Mississippi
Ballentine's Mississippi Regiment

*Ross' Brigade –
    Brigadier General Lawrence S. Ross*
5th Texas
6th Texas
9th Texas
1st Texas Legion

Artillery
(At Murfreesborough during Battle of Nashville)
Morton's Tennessee Battery

THE MARCH TO
THE SEA: PART 2

In the North, as November drew to a close, there was an atmosphere of unease. Hood was pushing deep into Tennessee while there was nothing but rumor and the occasional report from a Southern newspaper to give any indication of what was happening to Sherman's men. Lincoln had to trust in the reassurances from Grant that Sherman would be fine, and until communications were re-established when Sherman reached the coast, there could be no way of knowing what was happening in Georgia.

There was little cause for concern. The four corps were now closer together as they prepared to swing to the southeast and Savannah. Augusta was still threatened, a fact that had drawn Wheeler's cavalry across to defend the town and the important military works there. Kilpatrick, following his Confederate opponent, would press on toward Augusta to keep up the pretense that it was a target for the march. His actions would precipitate the fiercest fighting of the entire campaign.

A series of cavalry skirmishes commenced on the night of November 26, when Wheeler's men surprised Kilpatrick in camp. Barely escaping himself, "Little Kil" led his men in a series of fighting retreats, constantly pressed by Wheeler's troopers. Kilpatrick's official report briefly mentions a few unproductive attacks by Wheeler before he "deemed it prudent to retire to our infantry." In fact, Wheeler's attacks had repeatedly driven the Federals from their positions and they were relieved to fall back on the support of infantrymen. On November 28, confusion caused Kilpatrick and two cavalry regiments, the 8th Indiana and 9th Michigan, to be almost

An evocative depiction of the chaos wrought by Sherman's men on the March to the Sea, containing most of the defining elements – the destruction of the railroad, the burning of property, and the driving off of livestock, along with cavalry skirmishes, terrified civilians and liberated slaves. (LOC, LC-USZ62-7333)

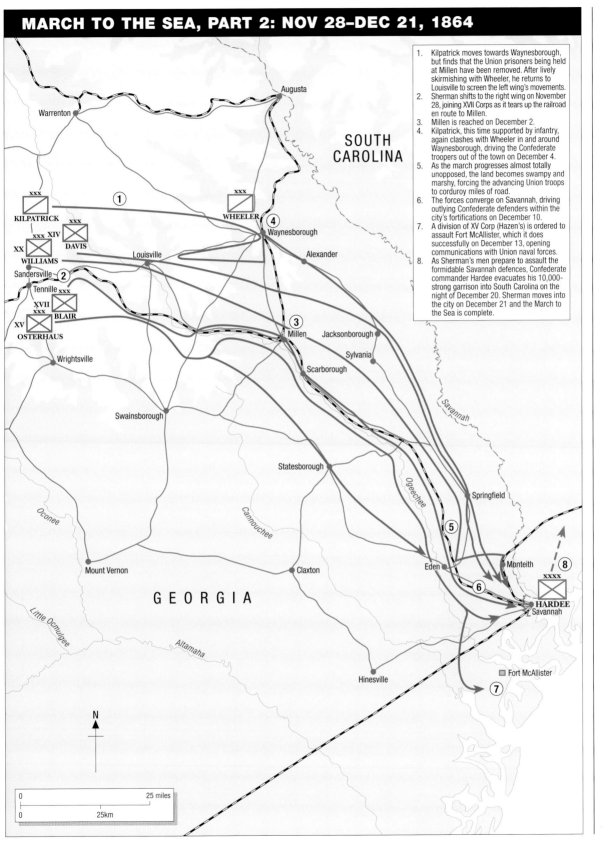

MARCH TO THE SEA, PART 2: NOV 28–DEC 21, 1864

SOUTH CAROLINA

GEORGIA

Augusta

Warrenton

KILPATRICK

WHEELER

Waynesborough

XIV

DAVIS

Alexander

XX

WILLIAMS

Louisville

Sandersville

Tennille

Millen

Jacksonborough

XVII

BLAIR

Sylvania

XV

OSTERHAUS

Scarborough

Wrightsville

Swainsborough

Statesborough

Springfield

Oconee

Cannouchee

Eden

Monteith

Mount Vernon

Claxton

HARDEE

Savannah

Little Ocmulgee

Altamaha

Hinesville

Fort McAllister

Savannah

Ogeechee

1. Kilpatrick moves towards Waynesborough, but finds that the Union prisoners being held at Millen have been removed. After lively skirmishing with Wheeler, he returns to Louisville to screen the left wing's movements.
2. Sherman shifts to the right wing on November 28, joining XVII Corps as it tears up the railroad en route to Millen.
3. Millen is reached on December 2.
4. Kilpatrick, this time supported by infantry, again clashes with Wheeler in and around Waynesborough, driving the Confederate troopers out of the town on December 4.
5. As the march progresses almost totally unopposed, the land becomes swampy and marshy, forcing the advancing Union troops to corduroy miles of road.
6. The forces converge on Savannah, driving outlying Confederate defenders within the city's fortifications on December 10.
7. A division of XV Corp (Hazen's) is ordered to assault Fort McAllister, which it does successfully on December 13, opening communications with Union naval forces.
8. As Sherman's men prepare to assault the formidable Savannah defences, Confederate commander Hardee evacuates his 10,000-strong garrison into South Carolina on the night of December 20. Sherman moves into the city on December 21 and the March to the Sea is complete.

N

0 ————————— 25 miles

0 ————————— 25km

This artist's impression of Sherman's headquarters on the march conveys his preference for simple living. Sherman disdained officers who brought large amounts of personal belongings with them on campaign and tried to set an example of frugality. (*Harper's Weekly*)

entirely surrounded by Confederate troopers and a desperate fight ensued before he was able to escape. Following these chaotic and fierce encounters, Kilpatrick took his cavalry corps to Louisville, where the men were able to rest for two days.

Kilpatrick and Wheeler would meet again, but for now the important work revolved around the familiar tasks of destroying the railroads and foraging. "On 27th, 28th and 29th," wrote Alpheus S. Williams, "the central railroad and all wagon bridges over Williamson's Swamp Creek were destroyed from Tennille Station to the Ogeechee River … by the First and Second Divisions and Michigan Engineers." In considering the amount of supplies gleaned from the country, Williams would admit that the wastage was "enormous," adding that "we swept, with our foragers and flankers, a belt of six to eight miles in width of all the cotton and most of the gins and presses."

The country was changing, the soil becoming sandy and marshy and the foraging less productive; "… after three miles of miserable pine swamp," wrote Captain Wills with the right wing, on November 26, "we crossed the Oconee on pontoons." On November 27 he wrote, "Have had a tedious march over sandy roads and through pine woods for 11 miles." Wills appears to have taken a great dislike to pine trees, complaining about the odor when pine knots were burned. The Illinoisan retained his sense of humor ("Lieutenant Dorrance swallowed his false teeth a few nights ago, and complains that they don't agree with him"), but by November 29 the march was beginning to lose its appeal. He wrote of spending all day in "an awful pine forest. I never saw such a lonesome place. Not a bird, not a sign of animal life, but the shrill notes of the tree frog. Not a twig of undergrowth, and no vegetable life but just grass and pitch pine."

On November 30 Wills' division passed through Summerville, where a German farmer was reduced to tears by the music of the 12th Indiana band as they marched past. "That is the first music I have heard for four years," he sobbed, "it makes me think of home. Damn this Georgia pine wood." A few hours later, hundreds of miles to the northwest, Hood lined his men up at Franklin.

THE BATTLE OF WAYNESBOROUGH

By December 1 Sherman considered that Kilpatrick's men had rested long enough and he instructed the cavalry commander to give Wheeler "all the fighting he wanted." The Federal horsemen rode out again, but this time they took Brigadier General Absalom Baird's 3rd Division, XIV Corps, along as support. This operation would no doubt have brought a wry smile to Wheeler's face – the Confederate commander had written rather pointedly that, having sought the protection of infantry in their earlier skirmishing, Kilpatrick "did not venture to forsake [that protection] again during the campaign, no doubt being too much demoralized to again meet our cavalry."

The combined Union force now moved in search of Wheeler. Skirmishing began again on December 1, 9 miles from Waynesborough. The following day a strong Confederate force was found on the opposite bank of Rocky Creek and was forced to withdraw by a joint assault of infantry and cavalry. On December 3, Baird's infantrymen began to tear up railroad track around Thomas' Station, under the watchful eye of the cavalry. Colonel Smith D. Atkins' 2nd Brigade of the cavalry division fought off several nighttime attacks from Wheeler.

The next day, Wheeler was entrenched outside Waynesborough. Dismounted cavalry resisted the first Union assault, but a subsequent attack forced the Confederates to fall back to a second line. This line was so long that Kilpatrick deemed an outflanking movement to be

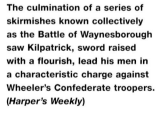

The culmination of a series of skirmishes known collectively as the Battle of Waynesborough saw Kilpatrick, sword raised with a flourish, lead his men in a characteristic charge against Wheeler's Confederate troopers. (*Harper's Weekly*)

Conditions inside the military prison at Millen were terrible, but Kilpatrick was unable to rescue the Union captives held there. "To my great regret, I learned that our prisoners had been removed two days previous," Kilpatrick would report. "It is needless to say that had this not been the case I should have rescued them. The Confederate Government could not have prevented me." (*Harper's Weekly*)

Anger over the conditions inside the military prison may have been a factor in the destruction wrought upon Millen. The prison, and much of the town, was burned. (*Harper's Weekly*)

impractical. He instead decided to break the line in the center. With the 8th Indiana dismounted and advancing as skirmishers, Kilpatrick sent four regiments forward (the 9th Pennsylvania on the left, the 3rd Kentucky in the center, and both the 5th and 2nd Kentucky on the right). Wheeler's men were routed and driven from the town, being pursued for 8 miles toward Augusta. Their defense, however, had been fierce, Kilpatrick reporting that 200 captured rebels bore saber wounds to testify to the strength of their resistance.

Sherman was delighted with Kilpatrick's success. "I beg to assure you that the operations of the cavalry under your command have been skilful and eminently successful," he wrote to his cavalry commander on receipt of his official report. The last major obstacle between Sherman and Savannah was removed with the defeat of Wheeler's cavalry. The Confederate horsemen followed the progressing Union corps towards Savannah, but could only harass the rearguard and flanks.

Kilpatrick had not attained one of his goals, though. The prisoners at Millen were moved before the Union troopers could rescue them. When the men of XVII Corps, with whom Sherman now traveled, entered Millen on December 2, they inspected the abandoned prison. The harshness of conditions at Camp Lawton was apparent from the scarcity of adequate shelter, the stocks used for punishing the prisoners and, most harrowing, the burial pit with the simple inscription "650 Buried Here." In a grim mood, the Federal soldiers burned much of Millen, including the prison.

The right wing of Sherman's army was enjoying a period of calm following Wheeler's shift of focus and the serious losses imposed on enemy forces at Griswoldville. On December 1 Captain Wills wrote of the distinctive flora and fauna on the march adding, "We have not heard a Rebel gun since the 22nd of last month. They don't trouble our march a particle." The third was a day of rest for Wills' Division, "our first rest since leaving Atlanta." News came to the right wing that Kilpatrick was moving on the railroad between Millen and Augusta, and the sound of cannon fire for two hours the next day signaled the final clash with Wheeler, but for the right wing it was a time of marching and speculation, not action. By December 5 talk had turned to how much damage the Union army had inflicted on the Confederacy since starting after Hood in October. "We all agree that the following estimate is not too high in any particular," wrote Wills. "100,000 hogs, 20,000 head of cattle, 15,000 horses and mules; 500,000 bushels of corn, 100,000 of sweet potatoes. We are driving with us many thousand of the cattle. The destruction of railroad property has been complete whenever within our reach."

Sherman was now convinced that he could not be prevented from reaching his goal. Confederate defenders at Savannah could not, by his estimation, number more than 10,000. After leaving Millen on December 4 he swung his army directly on Savannah, the time for pretense having passed. Three of his corps were now moving on the marshy land between the Ogeechee and Savannah rivers, slowing progress. Rebel defenders also sporadically blocked roads, but any delays were minor, as the defending soldiers were quickly outflanked and the pioneer battalions cleared obstructions. The mood of the commanding general was buoyant. "The weather was fine, the roads good, and every thing seemed to favor us," he would later write in his memoirs. "Never do I recall a more agreeable sensation than the sight of our camps by night, lit up by the fires of fragrant pine-knots. The trains were all in good order, and the men seemed to march their fifteen miles a day as though it were nothing."

In the Confederate ranks, pressure was mounting. Beauregard felt it necessary to defend his decision to concur with Hood's plan to invade Tennessee, writing on December 6 to President Davis that once Sherman's march had started it would have been futile to call Hood back to chase him over a devastated country offering no supplies for his army, and with every river crossing destroyed. Beauregard also pointed out that

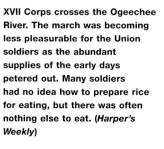

XVII Corps crosses the Ogeechee River. The march was becoming less pleasurable for the Union soldiers as the abundant supplies of the early days petered out. Many soldiers had no idea how to prepare rice for eating, but there was often nothing else to eat. (*Harper's Weekly*)

information had convinced him that a force of around 30,000 men could have been assembled to confront Sherman in Georgia. This figure would still have been inadequate, but Beauregard went on to claim that he had estimated Sherman's effective strength at just 36,000, inclusive of cavalry, a figure that was obviously hugely inaccurate. Beauregard also made the strange assertion that Sherman would "doubtless be prevented from capturing Augusta, Charleston, and Savannah, and he may yet be made to experience serious loss before reaching the coast." Sherman was in a position to capture whatever objective he chose to steer his columns towards, and the losses being inflicted on his army were paltry, although a new weapon in the Confederate arsenal would soon draw his wrath.

On December 8 Sherman rode up to a group of men by the roadside. They were gathered around a young officer whose leg had been terribly injured by an exploding torpedo. The primitive landmine had killed the officer's horse, blown off his right foot, and severely damaged his knee. The leg would have to be amputated.

"This was not war, but murder," Sherman fumed, "and it made me very angry." In a display of cold rage, Sherman called up a group of Confederate prisoners and, despite their protestations, forced them to advance along the road, probing with picks and spades for more torpedoes. "They begged hard," Sherman wrote, "but I reiterated the order and could hardly help laughing at their stepping so gingerly along the road … but they found no other torpedoes till near Fort McAllister."

The march was now nearing its goal, and things were becoming uncomfortable for the Union soldiers. The rich pickings of the early days of the march were a distant memory as the men tried to subsist on rice and the occasional slaughtered animal. For the advance units, miles from the supply trains, hunger was now intense. Happily for them, by December 10 the army was drawing up in front of Savannah.

FORT MCALLISTER

It was still not easy for the Union army to open communications with Union naval forces because the mouth of the Ogeechee was dominated by Fort McAllister. Originally constructed by slaves at the outbreak of the war and designed to hold just four guns, the fort had been expanded until it was now a formidable position, making it impossible for any naval vessels to pass by. The fort's thick, squat, earthen walls were able to absorb prolonged punishment from naval gunfire and could quickly be repaired. The fort was vulnerable from the landward side, however. Not having been constructed to withstand an infantry assault, the main guns faced Ossabaw Sound and the Ogeechee River.

Strangely, Sherman seems to have been concerned about the storming of the fort. With its garrison of just 130–150 men, it could not hope to stand for long against a determined infantry assault, but on selecting Brigadier General William B. Hazen of the 2nd Division, XV Corps, to carry out the attack, he was at pains to point out the importance of the job. "I explained to General Hazen," Sherman later wrote, "that on his action depended the safety of the whole army, and the success of the campaign." In choosing his former division, "the same old division which I had commanded at Shiloh and Vicksburg, in which I felt a special pride and

confidence," Sherman further betrayed his concern that the fort might offer stubborn resistance.

On December 13 Hazen advanced nine regiments to within 600 yards of the fort. The marshy ground made deployment difficult, but by 4.45pm the men were ready to attack. A line of skirmishers in advance of the main body was able to pick off many of the gun crews on the rear-facing guns inside the fort. Placed on barbettes, these guns were elevated above the walls, rather than firing through embrasures, making the crews serving the guns extremely vulnerable to sharpshooters.

From a nearby observation platform, Sherman watched. "The sun was rapidly declining, and I was dreadfully impatient," he wrote of the agonizing moments before the assault began. A US Navy steamer appeared and signaled to Sherman, asking who he was and whether Fort McAllister had been taken. Sherman's reply was "Not yet, but it will be in a minute!" and he wrote in his memoirs that "Almost at that instant of time, we saw Hazen's troops come out of the dark fringe of woods that encompassed the fort, the lines dressed as on parade, with colors flying, and moving forward with a quick, steady pace."

With the men widely spaced to limit the effectiveness of the defending artillery, the nine regiments started forward on the three landward sides of the fort. Outside the walls there was an extensive line of abatis, made by sharpened oak branches, with a deep ditch behind. There was also a line of buried torpedoes, which would be highly effective. Inside the fort were men of the Emmett Rifles, Clinch's light battery, and companies D and E of the 1st Georgia Reserves. Despite the attentions of the Union sharpshooters the garrison put up stiff resistance. "Fort McAllister was then all alive," Sherman observed, "its

FORT MCALLISTER, DECEMBER 13, 1864 (Pages 78–79)
Fort McAllister had originally been a four-gun emplacement to guard the entrance to the Ogeechee River and, thus, defend the "back door" into Savannah. It was steadily augmented throughout the war and its thick earthen walls proved capable of withstanding tremendous punishment from Union naval vessels, including ironclads. The beauty of the walls was that they could be easily repaired overnight, ready to renew battle the following day. The fort was not, however, designed to withstand an assault from the landward side, from where the men of Hazen's 2nd Division, XV Corps, approached on December 13, 1864. The Federals approached on three sides, with about 750 men of the 2nd Brigade approaching the northwest wall. The infantrymen were more widely spaced than usual to limit the effectiveness of the defending artillery (1) and sharpshooters picked off the Confederate gun crews from long range (2), so that there were almost no casualties among the attacking troops until they closed on the fort.

Here, there were substantial defensive works to cross. "Just outside the works a line of torpedoes had been placed," wrote Hazen in his official report, "many of which were exploded by the tread of the troops, blowing many men to atoms, but the line moved on without checking." (3). A deep ditch, abatis, and palisades were the next obstacles. A bridge over the ditch was guarded by a mountain howitzer (4), firing through a gap in the walls and therefore protected from the Union sharpshooters, but the obstacles were unable to hold up the attacking soldiers. The flag-bearers of the 47th Ohio (5) and 111th Illinois (6) vied to be the first to place their colors on the walls, eventually sharing the honor. As the assaulting troops stormed into the fort, savage hand-to-hand fighting broke out, with the garrison refusing to surrender despite the odds (7). The defenders' resistance was brave but futile – Fort McAllister had fallen in 15 minutes and Sherman's communications with Union naval forces were opened.

The men of 2nd Division, XV Corps, storm Fort McAllister in this artist's impression. "The conduct of the regiments engaged deserves the highest praise," wrote Colonel James S. Martin, commanding the 2nd Brigade. "Not a falter, but steadily on under a withering fire, until three starry banners waved from the parapets." (*Harper's Weekly*)

The heavy guns of Fort McAllister were removed by Union engineers after the capture of the fort, many of them intended for use in the siege of Savannah. Brigadier General William B. Hazen reported the capture of 24 guns, as well as substantial amounts of ammunition and supplies for the garrison. (LOC, LC-B811-3498)

big guns belching forth dense clouds of smoke, which soon enveloped our assaulting lines."

The Federals made best progress to the northwest wall, where the assaulting troops were soon pouring over the parapet. "Here," Hazen would report, "the fighting became desperate and deadly." The defenders refused to surrender, fighting on until they were killed, wounded, or simply overpowered by the huge numbers of Union troops pouring into the fort.

"There was a pause," Sherman wrote, "a cessation of fire; the smoke cleared away, and the parapets were blue with our men, who fired their muskets in the air and shouted so that we actually heard them, or felt that we did." It had taken just 15 minutes for the fort to fall. Hazen's casualties were reported as 24 officers and men killed, with a further 110 wounded, many of the casualties being caused by the buried torpedoes.

The US Navy steamer turned out to be the *Dandelion*, not the most warlike name for the ship that would establish a link between Sherman's command and the sea, but welcome nonetheless. Sherman planned to row out to her that evening, but first he visited Fort McAllister, congratulating Hazen on his success. Sherman was warned about the dangers of torpedoes, both around the fort and in Ossabaw Sound. As if to emphasize the danger, a Union soldier was blown to pieces by a buried torpedo while Sherman was at the fort. Still, eager for news from the outside world, Sherman was determined to reach the *Dandelion* that night.

On boarding the steamer, Sherman learned that "matters and things generally remained pretty much the same as when we had left Atlanta." Dashing off several hasty letters, including updates for Grant, Admiral John A. Dahlgren (the ranking naval officer in the area), and Secretary of War Edwin M. Stanton, he then returned to Fort McAllister. The letters were substantially the same, sketching the events of the past month and ending with the triumphant declaration: "I regard Savannah as already gained."

THE FATE OF SAVANNAH

Sherman's elation was premature. Grant had plans that did not include the taking of Savannah and instead entailed shifting the bulk of Sherman's army to help with the campaign against Lee. This deflating news appears to have shocked Sherman, who could see his march ending in an anti-climax. There was further sobering news from Nashville. Thomas had fallen back on his defenses and was, apparently, doing nothing. "I have said all I can to force him to attack, without giving the positive order until to-day [December 6]," wrote Grant. "To-day, however, I could stand it no longer, and gave the order without any reserve."

Sherman could not know that Thomas had moved, spectacularly, by December 16, and his reply to Grant on that date included the not wholly flattering observation that "General Thomas is slow in mind and in action; but he is judicious and brave, and the troops feel great confidence in him." Of more concern to Sherman, however, was the possible derailment of his plans. Ever the good soldier, he started to formulate plans to concur with Grant's wishes. Fort McAllister would be used as a base to gather the elements of his army for transfer – the cavalry and artillery would remain, with a sufficient infantry force to protect them. Colonel Poe was instructed to scout out the area around Fort McAllister to make sure it was a suitable staging post.

Sherman knew, however, that logistical reality could yet work in his favor. It would take time for the necessary transports for 50,000 men to be assembled. If, in the meantime, he could take Savannah, he would not be disobeying orders. Grant may have believed that "the most important operation toward closing out the rebellion will be to close out Lee and his army," but Sherman was convinced that a further march, through the Carolinas, would be a surer way of hastening the end of the war. His reply to Grant included the throwaway remark that he had "initiated measures

Admiral John A. Dahlgren, posing here in front of the gun of his own design, made an immediate impression on Sherman when the two met following the fall of Fort McAllister. "I was not personally acquainted with him at the time," Sherman recalled, "but he was so extremely kind and courteous that I was at once attracted to him." (LOC, LC-B811-3417)

looking principally to coming to you with fifty or sixty thousand infantry, and incidentally to capture Savannah, if time will allow." Meetings with Dahlgren (with whom Sherman struck up an immediate rapport) and Major General John G. Foster, commander of the Department of the South, took care of the need to resupply his army and Sherman turned his attention to taking Savannah.

This could yet prove a difficult task. Under Hardee the Confederates had scraped together a small garrison, but a potentially effective one when the strong defensive position of the city was also considered. With extensive marshlands to Savannah's rear, Sherman's approach to the city was difficult. The defenders could flood the rice fields at will by opening floodgates and there was a line of substantial breastworks, parapets, and artillery emplacements. Approximately 10,000 troops manned the defensive line, split into three sections. Smith's militia force held the extreme right of the line, with a division under Lafayette McLaws in the center. The left was held by a division under the command of Major General Ambrose R. Wright. A total of 81 pieces of artillery were distributed fairly evenly along the length of the line.

A stubborn resistance by this patchwork force could inflict heavy casualties on an assaulting army, although the final outcome would be in little doubt considering the size of the Union army. A lack of heavy guns (Sherman's men had marched with only light artillery) would hold up proceedings until they could be brought into the siege lines, but Sherman was aware that delays were undesirable given Grant's new instructions. When he contacted the commander of the Savannah garrison on December 17, therefore, he tried to bluster his way into the city. Demanding immediate surrender, he threatened that:

should I be forced to resort to assault, or the slower and surer process of starvation, I shall then feel justified in resorting to the harshest measures, and shall make little effort to restrain my army – burning to avenge the national wrong which they attach to Savannah and other large cities which have been so prominent in dragging our country into civil war.

Sherman's threats do not reflect much credit on him, and Hardee's dignified refusal to surrender should have caused him some chagrin. The fact was, however, that plans were already under way to evacuate the city – a pontoon bridge was being constructed over the Savannah River and on December 18 Beauregard issued a "Memorandum for location of troops," outlining where the different elements of the garrison were to head for after evacuating the city. The next day a detailed timetable for the withdrawal, under cover of darkness, was issued. Wheeler's cavalry would cover the retreat, to take place on the night of December 20.

The retreat would be just in time – 30lb Parrott guns were on their way to Sherman, who wrote once more to Grant on December 18, ending with an impassioned plea to be able to continue on his destructive course:

With Savannah in our possession … we can punish South Carolina as she deserves, and as thousands of the people in Georgia hoped we would do. I do sincerely believe that the whole United States, North and South, would rejoice to have this army turned loose on South Carolina, to dev-astate that State in the manner we have done in Georgia, and it would have a direct and immediate bearing on your campaign in Virginia.

While awaiting a reply, Sherman made belated efforts to complete the investment of Savannah. He was well aware that a narrow escape route existed and started to formulate plans to close it. On the night of December 20, however, the Confederate army evacuated the city. Union troops from Slocum's left wing moved in the next morning and Sherman himself followed on December 22. The city was eerily calm. The Confederate ram *Savannah* and the naval yard were burning, but

Dec 25

In a playful telegram, Sherman offered Savannah to Lincoln "as a Christmas gift ... with 150 heavy guns and plenty of ammunition and also about 25,000 bales of cotton." Lincoln's reply was heartfelt: "many, many thanks... the honor is all yours." (National Archives)

there were few other signs of destruction. On Christmas Eve news of Thomas' smashing victory at Nashville reached the Union troops in Savannah. Sherman had already entered into the seasonal spirit by offering the city of Savannah to Lincoln as a Christmas gift and he now wrote a warm congratulatory message to Thomas.

His troops were the next to bask in Sherman's good humor. On January 8, Special Orders No. 6 was issued to the men who had marched with him, detailing their triumphant achievements and adding:

> Almost at the moment of our victorious entry into Savannah came the welcome and expected news that our comrades in Tennessee had also fulfilled nobly and well their part… So complete a success in military operations, extending over half a continent, is an achievement that entitles it to a place in the military history of the world.

Sherman's army had lost a total of just 1,888 men, killed, wounded, missing, or captured. A total of 13,294 head of cattle had been captured along the way, along with around 7,000 horses and mules. Nearly ten million pounds of corn had been commandeered, and over 300 miles of railroad destroyed. The exact dollar amount of damage can only be estimated, which Sherman himself did at $100,000,000, a staggering amount for 19th-century America. Only a fifth of that was, in Sherman's words, "inured to our advantage, and the remainder is simple waste and destruction."

The health of the men on the march was also remarkable. Assistant Surgeon David L. Huntington reported only 32 deaths from disease, and an average of just 1.9 percent of the men were unfit for duty at any given time on the march. This no doubt had much to do with the weeding-out process undertaken before the march began, which removed 748 sickly

soldiers, "the greater portion of whom were recruits suffering from measles and diseases incident to newly enlisted men," Huntington would comment. The nature of the campaign was also beneficial to the men's health, and Sherman now intended to give his men more fresh air and exercise.

Sherman had already received a communication from Grant, informing him of another change of mind from his superior – Sherman could now continue as he wished, laying waste to the Carolinas en route to linking up with Grant to trap Lee and the last remaining Confederate army in an inescapable vice. With great satisfaction Sherman planned his next move. As he wrote in his memoirs, "Here terminated the 'March to the Sea.'" In many ways, however, Sherman's work had just begun.

Union soldiers in captured Savannah set up a newspaper, called the *Daily Loyal Georgian*, publishing the first issue on Christmas Eve, 1864. Among other stories and announcements was news of the stunning Union victory at Nashville. (*Harper's Weekly*)

ORDERS OF BATTLE

THE MARCH TO THE SEA, NOVEMBER 15–DECEMBER 21, 1864

UNION FORCES
Overall command: Major General William Tecumseh Sherman

Headquarters Guard
7th Company Ohio Sharpshooters

Engineers
1st Missouri (five companies)

The Army of the Tennessee (right wing)
Commander:
    Major General Oliver O. Howard
Approximately 27,000 men

Escort
15th Illinois Cavalry, Company K
4th Company Ohio Cavalry

XV Corps
Major General Peter J. Osterhaus
(15,679 men)

1st Division
Brigadier General Charles R. Woods

1st Brigade – Colonel Milo Smith
12th Indiana
26th Iowa
27th Missouri
29th Missouri
31st & 32nd Missouri Battalion
76th Ohio

2nd Brigade – Brigadier General Charles C. Walcutt (wounded Nov 22)/
    Colonel Robert F. Catterson
26th Illinois
40th Illinois
103rd Illinois
97th Indiana
100th Indiana
6th Iowa
46th Ohio

3rd Brigade – Colonel James A. Williamson
4th Iowa
9th Iowa
25th Iowa
30th Iowa
31st Iowa

2nd Division
Brigadier General William B. Hazen

1st Brigade – Colonel Theodore Jones
55th Illinois
116th Illinois
127th Illinois
6th Missouri
8th Missouri (two companies)
30th Ohio
57th Ohio

2nd Brigade – Colonel Wells S. Jones
    (wounded Dec 13)/Colonel James S. Martin
111th Illinois
83rd Indiana
37th Ohio
47th Ohio
53rd Ohio
54th Ohio
3rd Brigade – Colonel John M. Oliver
48th Illinois
90th Illinois
99th Indiana
15th Michigan
70th Ohio

3rd Division
Brigadier General John E. Smith

1st Brigade – Colonel Joseph B. McCown
63rd Illinois
93rd Illinois (non-veterans 18th Wisconsin attached)
48th Indiana
59th Indiana
4th Minnesota

2nd Brigade –
    Bvt Brigadier General Green B. Raum
56th Illinois
10th Iowa
26th Missouri (detachment 10th Missouri attached)
80th Ohio

4th Division
Brigadier General John M. Corse

1st Brigade –
    Brigadier General Elliott W. Rice
52nd Illinois
66th Indiana
2nd Iowa
7th Iowa

2nd Brigade – Colonel Robert N. Adams
12th Illinois
66th Illinois
81st Ohio

3rd Brigade –
    Lieutenant Colonel Frederick J. Hurlbut
7th Illinois
50th Illinois
57th Illinois
39th Iowa

Artillery
Major Charles J. Stolbrand

1st Illinois Light, Battery H
1st Michigan Light, Battery B
1st Missouri Light, Battery H
Wisconsin Light, 12th Battery

XVII Corps
Major General Frank P. Blair, Jr.
(11,358 men)

Escort
11th Illinois Cavalry, Company G

1st Division
Major General Joseph A. Mower

1st Brigade –
    Brigadier General John W. Fuller
64th Illinois
18th Missouri
27th Ohio
39th Ohio

2nd Brigade –
    Brigadier General John W. Sprague
35th New Jersey
43rd Ohio
63rd Ohio
25th Wisconsin

3rd Brigade – Colonel John Tillson
10th Illinois
25th Indiana
32nd Wisconsin

3rd Division
Brigadier General Mortimer D. Leggett

Provost Guard
20th Illinois, Captain Henry King

1st Brigade –
    Brigadier General Manning F. Force
30th Illinois
31st Illinois
45th Illinois
12th Wisconsin
16th Wisconsin

2nd Brigade – Colonel Robert K. Scott
20th Ohio
68th Ohio
78th Ohio
17th Wisconsin

4th Division
Brigadier General Giles A. Smith

1st Brigade – Colonel Benjamin F. Potts
14th Illinois (Battalion)
15th Illinois
41st Illinois (Battalion)
53rd Illinois
23rd Indiana
53rd Indiana
32nd Ohio

Third Brigade –
  Brigadier General William W. Belknap
32nd Illinois
11th Iowa
13th Iowa
15th Iowa
16th Iowa

Artillery
1st Michigan Light, Battery C
Minnesota Light, 1st Battery
Ohio Light, 15th Battery

The Army of Georgia (left wing)

Commander:
  Major General Henry W. Slocum
(Approximately 27,500 men)

Pontoniers
58th Indiana

Engineers
1st Michigan (detachment)

XIV Corps

Bvt Major General Jefferson C. Davis
(13,352 men)

1st Division
Brigadier General William P. Carlin

1st Brigade – Colonel Harrison C. Hobart
104th Illinois
42nd Indiana
88th Indiana
33rd Ohio
94th Ohio
21st Wisconsin

2nd Brigade –
  Lieutenant Colonel Joseph H. Brigham
13th Michigan
21st Michigan
69th Ohio

3rd Brigade – Colonel Henry A. Hambright
  (sick from 18 Nov)/
  Lieutenant Colonel David Miles
38th Indiana
21st Ohio
74th Ohio
79th Pennsylvania

2nd Division
Brigadier General James D. Morgan

1st Brigade – Colonel Robert F. Smith
16th Illinois
60th Illinois
10th Michigan
14th Michigan
17th New York

2nd Brigade –
  Lieutenant Colonel John S. Pearce
34th Illinois
78th Illinois
98th Ohio
108th Ohio
113th Ohio
121st Ohio

3rd Brigade –
  Lieutenant Colonel James W. Langley
85th Illinois

86th Illinois
110th Illinois
125th Illinois
22nd Indiana
52nd Ohio

3rd Division
Brigadier General Absalom Baird

1st Brigade – Colonel Morton C. Hunter
82nd Indiana
23rd Missouri
17th Ohio
31st Ohio
89th Ohio
92nd Ohio (Company A, 24th Illinois
  attached)

2nd Brigade – Colonel Newell Gleason
75th Indiana
87th Indiana
101st Indiana
2nd Minnesota
105th Ohio

3rd Brigade – Colonel George P. Este
74th Indiana
18th Kentucky
14th Ohio
38th Ohio

Artillery
Major Charles Houghtaling
1st Illinois Light, Battery C (detachment 11th
  Ohio infantry attached)
2nd Illinois Light, Battery I
Indiana Light, 19th Battery
Wisconsin Light, 5th Battery

XX Corps

Brigadier General Alpheus S. Williams
(14,096 men)

1st Division
Brigadier General Nathaniel J. Jackson

1st Brigade – Colonel James L. Selfridge
5th Connecticut
123rd New York
141st New York
46th Pennsylvania

2nd Brigade – Colonel Ezra A. Carman
2nd Massachusetts
13th New Jersey
107th New York
150th New York
3rd Wisconsin

3rd Brigade – Colonel James S. Robinson
82nd Illinois
101st Illinois
143rd New York
61st Ohio
82nd Ohio
31st Wisconsin

2nd Division
Brigadier General John W. Geary

1st Brigade – Colonel Ario Pardee, Jr.
5th Ohio
29th Ohio
66th Ohio
28th Pennsylvania
147th Pennsylvania (detachment Battery E,
  Pennsylvania Artillery, attached)

2nd Brigade – Colonel Patrick H. Jones
33rd New Jersey
119th New York
134th New York
154th New York
73rd Pennsylvania
109th Pennsylvania

3rd Brigade – Colonel Henry A. Barnum
60th New York
102nd New York
137th New York
149th New York
29th Pennsylvania
111th Pennsylvania

3rd Division
Brigadier General William T. Ward

1st Brigade – Colonel Franklin C. Smith
102nd Illinois
105th Illinois
129th Illinois
70th Indiana
79th Ohio

2nd Brigade – Colonel Daniel Dustin
33rd Indiana
85th Indiana
19th Michigan
22nd Wisconsin

3rd Brigade – Colonel Samuel Ross
20th Connecticut
33rd Massachusetts
136th New York
55th Ohio
73rd Ohio
26th Wisconsin

Artillery
Major John A. Reynolds

1st New York Light, Battery I
1st New York Light, Battery M
1st Ohio Light, Battery C
Pennsylvania Light, Battery E

Cavalry
3rd Division
Brigadier General Judson Kilpatrick
(5,015 men)

1st Brigade – Colonel Eli H. Murray
8th Indiana
2nd Kentucky
3rd Kentucky
5th Kentucky
9th Pennsylvania

2nd Brigade – Colonel Smith D. Atkins
92nd Illinois
3rd Indiana
9th Michigan
5th Ohio
9th Ohio
10th Ohio
McLaughlin's (Ohio) Squadron

Unattached
1st Alabama Cavalry
9th Illinois Mounted Infantry

Artillery
Captain Yates V. Beebe

10th Wisconsin Battery

CONFEDERATE FORCES

Cavalry Corps
Commander: Major General Joseph Wheeler
(Approximately 3,500 men)

(No orders of battle are available for
Wheeler's cavalry force in the Savannah
campaign. A non-official order of battle has
been compiled using information gleaned
from official reports and other documents.)

The following brigades are mentioned by
Wheeler in his official report, or documented
in other sources:

Hannon's Brigade –
Colonel Moses W. Hannon

Lewis' Brigade –
Brigadier General Joseph H. Lewis

Dibrell's Brigade –
Brigadier General George G. Dibrell

Anderson's Brigade –
Lieutenant Colonel Anderson

Harrison's Texas Brigade –
Colonel Thomas Harrison

Ashby's Brigade –
Colonel Henry M. Ashby

Crews' Georgia Brigade –
Colonel Charles C. Crews

Hagan's Alabama Brigade –
Colonel James Hagan

Breckinridge's Brigade –
Colonel William C. P. Breckinridge

Ferguson's Brigade –
Brigadier General Samuel W. Ferguson

1st Division Georgia State Militia
Major General Gustavus W. Smith

1st Brigade Georgia State Militia
1st Georgia Militia
2nd Georgia Militia
3rd Georgia Militia

2nd Brigade Georgia State Militia
4th Georgia Militia
5th Georgia Militia
6th Georgia Militia

3rd Brigade Georgia State Militia
7th Georgia Militia
8th Georgia Militia
9th Georgia Militia

4th Brigade Georgia State Militia
10th Georgia Militia
11th Georgia Militia
12th Georgia Militia

**Additional forces with 2nd, 3rd, and 4th
Brigades, Georgia State Militia, at
Griswoldville, November 22, 1864**

*Georgia State Line – Lieutenant Colonel
Beverly D. Evans*
(two understrength regiments, approximately
400 men)
1st Georgia State Line
2nd Georgia State Line

*Confederate Reserve – Major Ferdinand
W. C. Cook*
(two battalions of the Confederate Reserve,
totaling around 400 men)
Athens Battalion
Augusta Battalion
14th Georgia Light Artillery, Anderson's
Battery (four guns)

Garrison of Savannah
Lieutenant General William J. Hardee
In addition to elements of Gustavus W.
Smith's Militia Division (holding the right of
the defensive works), the following units
were present in the garrison of Savannah:

McLaws' Division
Major General Lafayette McLaws

1st Georgia Regulars
Barnwell's (Georgia) Light Artillery
22nd Georgia Battalion (six companies)
27th Georgia Battalion, Company D
29th Georgia Battalion Cavalry (six
companies)
3rd South Carolina Cavalry (eight
companies)
Symons' Reserves (ten companies)
Beaufort (South Carolina) Artillery
Bonaud's (Georgia) Battalion (two
companies)
Terrell (Georgia) Light Artillery
Clinch's (Georgia) Light Artillery (two
companies)
Cobb Guards (two companies)
Daniell's (Georgia) Light Battery
Guerard's (Georgia) Light Battery
Maxwell's (Georgia) Light Battery
German (South Carolina) Artillery
Hanleiter's (Georgia) Battery
South Carolina Horse Artillery (section)
Lafayette (South Carolina) Artillery
Mercer (Georgia) Artillery
2nd Engineer Troops, Company D

Left wing
Major General Ambrose R. Wright

Colonel Browne's Local Brigade
Major Jackson's Augusta Battalion
Major Adams' Athens Battalion
1st Regiment Augusta Local Infantry
Clemon's Battalion Augusta Local Infantry
Jackson's Battalion Augusta Local Infantry
Brooks' Foreign Battalion
Griffin's detachment, 55th Georgia
Captain Barnes' company of artillerists from
Augusta
Colonel von Zinken's Local Troops
Ferguson's Brigade (dismounted)
Local Reserves from Savannah
Brooks' Light Battery
Guerard's Light Battery
Maxwell's & Barnwell's Light Batteries
(sections)
Major Hamilton's artillery battalion (detachment)

Further Artillery
Regular Light Battery
Anderson's Light Battery

Abell's Light Battery
Pruden's Light Battery

Other units
*Young's Brigade – Brigadier General Pierce
M. B. Young*
7th Georgia Cavalry
Cobb's (Georgia) Legion Cavalry
Phillips' (Georgia) Legion Cavalry
Jeff Davis Legion Cavalry

Garrison of Fort McAllister
Emmett Rifles
Clinch's Light Battery (section)
1st Georgia Reserves, Company D
1st Georgia Reserves, Company E

AFTERMATH

The damage done on Sherman's March to the Sea was purely temporary. Barns could be rebuilt, crops replanted, and railroads repaired. The psychological impact should also not be overestimated. As evidenced in the tales of defiant Southerners watching the Yankees pass by, the destruction wrought in Georgia probably did as much to harden hearts as break spirits. The march was, however, a clear sign that the war had passed a critical point. The conflict was no longer an evenly balanced contest; the advantages enjoyed by the North in terms of manpower and industrial capacity were manifesting themselves in the field and it was no longer possible to imagine a scenario in which the Confederacy could prevail.

Equally important in this respect, though often underestimated, was the work done by Thomas at Nashville. The routing of Hood's Army of Tennessee removed a major Confederate force from the map of the war, securing Sherman's rear in the process. In 1865 Hood was at Tupelo, Mississippi, with his battered men. He offered his resignation on January 13 and it was accepted.

Just days before, Lincoln, re-elected on November 8, 1864, was making an ominous speech to Congress, a speech in which he pointed

Union forces cross Broad River, South Carolina, on a pontoon bridge. In awful weather, Sherman's men kept up a steady pace of 10 miles a day and inflicted far more damage on the state than had been visited on Georgia. (*Harper's Weekly*)

The destruction of Hood's army was a major blow to the Confederate war effort. The climactic charge against Compton (now Shy's) Hill on the second day of the Battle of Nashville is captured by Howard Pyle in this dramatic painting. 'My line of advance lay across a cornfield, through every foot of which the men were exposed to a direct fire from the line of works in front and cross-fire on either flank,' wrote Colonel Lucius F. Hubbard of the 5th Minnesota. 'But seemingly unmindful of the storm of missiles they were breasting, the veterans of the Second Brigade did not falter.' (Minnesota Historical Society)

out that while the South was exhausting its resources, the North was actually becoming stronger. "We have more men now than we had when the war began," he stated. "We are gaining strength, and may, if need be, maintain the contest indefinitely," but Nathan Bedford Forrest's chilling words to his men on the disastrous close of the Tennessee campaign were evidence that the Confederacy was not yet finished:

> Be not allured by the siren song of peace, for there can be no peace save upon your separate independent nationality. You can never again unite with those who have murdered your sons, outraged your helpless families, and with demonic malice wantonly destroyed your property, and now seek to make slaves of you.

Sherman's march had apparently not quelled Southern fighting spirit, but then again he was far from done. Lee's Army of Virginia effectively stood alone against the North, with the Carolinas his vital supply base. On February 1, 1865, Sherman's 60,000 men began to march through South Carolina, organized in much the same way as on the March to the Sea, with Slocum and Howard again in charge of the two wings. "This campaign may properly be classed as a continuance of the former," Sherman wrote, but the destruction was far more severe than during the march through Georgia, partly because the Union soldiers saw South Carolina as the

XIV Corps crosses Juniper Creek, South Carolina, in March 1865. The logistical effort involved in the march through the Carolinas eclipsed that of the more famous March to the Sea, but Sherman was unable to bring his army to link up with Grant before Lee was forced to surrender, effectively ending the war. (*Harper's Weekly*)

hotbed of secessionism. The destruction obscured what was an incredible logistical feat in covering 10 miles a day through one of the worst winters in South Carolina's history. Nine major rivers and countless tributaries were bridged by Sherman's pioneer battalions. Sherman had followed his familiar and effective strategy of aiming for two key objectives, in this case Augusta and Charleston, before marching straight between them to his true objective, in this case Columbia.

Columbia became a symbol of the destructiveness of Sherman's troops. Occupied on February 17, half of the city was entirely destroyed by the next day. Blame was probably shared between drunken Union soldiers, freed slaves, departing rebel cavalry, and the weather itself – a strong wind exacerbating the fires, however they had started. Sherman himself helped with the serious attempts to control the fires during the night of February 17.

Sherman's men continued into North Carolina, but no longer in the destructive spirit with which they had marched through South Carolina. Confederate forces under Joseph E. Johnston, including still defiant regiments from the Army of Tennessee, made an attempt to slow Sherman's progress near Bentonville on March 19. The rebels were beaten, but Sherman chose not to pursue his weakened adversary, who was, after all, unable even to alter the route of the Federals' march.

The ultimate aim of Sherman was to link up with Grant to the north and crush Lee from both sides, but although his men had marched prodigiously for months, they had not marched quickly enough. By April 9 Grant had broken the Army of Virginia on his own, and the war was effectively over.

"Glory to God and our country," wrote Sherman in Special Orders No. 54, "and all honor to our comrades in arms, to whom we are marching! A little more labor, a little more toil on our part, the great race is won, and our Government stands regenerated, after four long years of war."

THE BATTLEFIELD TODAY

GEORGIA

Giving visitors insight into the experiences of Georgians during the Civil War is the work of the Georgia Civil War Heritage Trails organization. Two historic trails are being created (more are planned), with markers to illuminate key sites along the way. The March to the Sea Heritage Trail is of most interest in the context of this book, although the Atlanta Campaign Heritage Trail adds valuable background information.

Work on the March to the Sea Heritage Trail commenced in 2002 with the dedication of the first site marker, at the Immaculate Conception Church in Atlanta. A second marker was placed at the City Hall in Macon and a third along the route of Sherman's right wing, at Pine Barren Crossroads in Emanuel County. The Confederate Powder Works at Augusta, though not central to the story of the march, offers further insight into Civil War Georgia.

One of the few military actions of the campaign is commemorated at Fort McAllister, which has been preserved and is in excellent condition. Various events are staged at the fort each year, with the highlight being December's re-enactment of the storming of the fort, offering the chance to talk to Confederate "defenders" as they prepare for the coming battle. This is followed by an atmospheric candlelit tour of the fort. Camping sites and cabins are available for those wishing to make a longer stay at the site. The majestic house in which Sherman made his headquarters at Savannah, now called the Green-Meldrim Home, is open to visitors at a cost of $3 for adults and $2 for children.

TENNESSEE

The site of the Battle of Franklin has fallen victim to urban expansion and much of the Union lines has now been built over, but echoes of the battle remain. The Carter House, purchased by the State of Tennessee in 1951 and opened to the public in 1953, still bears the bullet holes from November 30, 1864. The Battle of Nashville site has also been swallowed up by the expanding city, but some key areas are still available for visits. Fort Negley, whose siege guns opened the battle on December 15, is now open to the public for the first time in 60 years, and there is no entrance fee. Shy's Hill (formerly Compton Hill) can be climbed more easily since a new pathway was opened, and there is still evidence of the Confederate trench works at the top of the hill. Redoubt No. 1, a key point of the first day's fighting at Nashville, has some useful interpretative signage.

BIBLIOGRAPHY

Davis, Burke, *Sherman's March* (New York, Vintage Books, 1988). A detailed account of
the social cost of Sherman's March.

Davis, George B. *et al.*, *The Official Military Atlas of the Civil War* (New York, Barnes &
Noble, 2003). Originally published 1891–1895.

Grant, Ulysses S., *Personal Memoirs* (New York, Modern Library, 1999).

Groom, Winston, *Shrouds of Glory: From Atlanta to Nashville: The Last Great Campaign
of the Civil War* (New York, Grove Press, 1995).

Horn, Stanley F., *The Decisive Battle of Nashville* (Baton Rouge, Louisiana State University
Press, 1956).

Jones, Charles Colcock, *The Siege of Savannah in December, 1864* (Albany, 1874).
Electronic edition: http://docsouth.unc.edu/jonescharles/jones.html. Valuable for
details of Confederate forces in Georgia.

McDonough, James L., *Five Tragic Hours: The Battle of Franklin* (Knoxville, University of
Tennessee Press, 1983). An unrivaled account of the Battle of Franklin.

McPherson, James M., *Battle Cry of Freedom* (Oxford, Oxford University Press, 1990).
The outstanding single-volume history of the Civil War.

Nevin, David, *Sherman's March* (Alexandria, Time-Life Books, 1986).

Reid, Brian Holden, *The American Civil War* (London, Cassell & Co.,1999).

Sherman, William T., *Memoirs of General William T. Sherman* (New York, Da Capo Press,
1984). Originally published 1875.

Sword, Wiley, *Embrace an Angry Wind: The Confederacy's Last Hurrah: Spring Hill,
Franklin and Nashville* (New York, HarperCollins, 1992).

Wills, Charles W., *Army Life of an Illinois Soldier* (Southern Illinois, Southern Illinois
University, 1996). Originally published 1906.

Zimmerman, Mark, *Guide to Civil War Nashville* (Nashville, Battle of Nashville Preservation
Society 2004).

US Government Printing Office, *The War of the Rebellion: A Compilation of the Official
Records of the Union and Confederate Armies* (Washington DC, 1889–91). Series I,
Volume XLIV. 'Operations in South Carolina, Georgia and Florida, Nov 14–Dec 31, 1864'

US Government Printing Office, *The War of the Rebellion: A Compilation of the Official
Records of the Union and Confederate Armies* (Washington DC, 1889–91). Series I,
Volume XLV. 'Operations in Kentucky, Southwest Virginia, Tennessee, Mississippi,
Alabama, and North Georgia, Nov 14 1864–Jan 23 1865'

Useful Websites

Georgia Civil War Heritage Trails http://www.gcwht.org
Fort McAllister http://www.fortmcallister.org
Battle of Nashville Preservation Society http://www.bonps.org
Save the Franklin Battle Field http://www.franklin-stfb.org
The Carter House, Franklin http://www.carter-house.org/

INDEX

95

96